AROUND THE WORLD IN SEVENTY YEARS

DECAMPING COMMUNISM FOR THE OTHER SIDE OF THE IRON CURTAIN

RAOUL M FISCHER

Copyright © 2020 by Raoul M. Fischer

All rights reserved.

Published by Firebrand Publishing Atlanta, GA USA

No part of this book may be reproduced in any form or by any electronic or mechanical means, including information storage and retrieval systems, without written permission from the author, except for the use of brief quotations in a book review and certain other noncommercial uses permitted by copyright law.

For permission requests, write to the publisher, addressed "Attention: Permissions coordinator," at the email address: support@firebrandpublishing.com

Limit of Liability/Disclaimer of Warranty: While the publisher and author have used their best efforts in preparing this book, they make no representations or warranties with respect to the accuracy or completeness of the contents of this book and specifically disclaim any implied warranties of merchantability or fitness for a particular purpose. No warranty may be created or extended by sales representatives or written sales materials. The advice and strategies contained herein may not be suitable for your situation. You should consult with a professional where appropriate. Neither the publisher nor the author shall be liable for damages arising here from.

Firebrand Publishing publishes in a variety of print and electronic formats and by print-on-demand. For more information about Firebrand Publishing products, visit https://firebrandpublishing.com

ISBN: 978-1-941907-23-8 (hardcover)

ISBN: 978-1-941907-24-5 (ebook)

Printed in the United States of America

CONTENTS

Introduction	vii
1. The Happiest Day In Their Life	1
2. Why Zagreb?	7
3. German Engineers build mines	11
4. Nazis taking over	14
5. From One Dictatorship, to Another, to a Third	20
6. Early Days Behind the Iron Curtain	30
7. The First Exposure to a Real Job	45
8. Looking At New Opportunities	54
9. Public Enemy	67
10. Controlling the Masses	74
11. Big Toe, Slowly, in Capitalism	83
12. America, Here We Come	99
13. Second Time In Hong Kong	103
14. The Land of Rising Sun	109
15. Back in the States	126
16. Life After Death	140
17. Post-Jadranka	146
18. A New Era	150
Timeline	155
Family Tree	159
Maps	161
Index of names	165

A Coronavirus Trip Into The Past

A Memoir

INTRODUCTION

Authors of memoirs, biographies, and historical works, all settle on a period they want to cover. This is a covenant with the reader, unless it's an autobiography where the protagonist, the writer eventually dies, time limits do not exist. To explain an event, or motives or drives, how far back in the history would one go?

Or, how far in the future must one venture, to show the impact of our subject on subsequent events? This work, being my memoir, will show the future well defined by my eventual demise. I will have to look into the past, but how far? Only as far as the available information about the family would allow me. That regrettably means not beyond my grandparents era.

As an immigrant to the United States nearly forty years ago, I decided to use that special status to build upon a story, of a guy who did well. But, looking at the numbers, there is nothing special in being a recent immigrant. Around 14% of today's US citizens have been like me, born outside of the United States.

I'm not talking about the times of mass emigration from Europe and Asia due to religious persecution or economic woes (in 1910, the number was a similar 15%). This is the twenty-first century and we are still seeing *"huddled masses yearning to breathe free"*[1].

This is no longer the best description of the cross-section of today's immigrants. A computer engineer, a medical doctor from India, a PhD from Japan, or nurses from the Philippines, are intermingled with economic migration from the south. In times past, 'The Land of the Free' was the clarion call. Today it's more, 'The Land of Opportunity', or at least a mixture of the two, especially valid for Central American immigration, where people are fleeing both domestic terror and poverty.

For me, the "free" could have been achieved in Western Europe without the swim across the Atlantic Ocean. So in my case, despite coming from a communist country, it was the call of opportunity that resonated for me. By the time I landed in Philadelphia, I wasn't apart of the communist system for over ten years. From 1972 I worked for an American company stationed in Switzerland and moved on, to the Far East, to eventually land in the United States in 1982.

So far, I've briefly addressed the timeframe and the environment. But the bigger question is: Why do it at all? My contributions to the world are hardly earth-shattering. I didn't invent anything of consequence, I didn't do anything to change the course of history or the world, and I didn't influence any improvement of the morale and ethics of my surroundings. I wasn't Atlas or Icarus. But, since almost all autobiographies and memoirs are written primarily for the benefit of the writer, this one will fall in the same category.

Since I lived in "interesting times", as the Chinese proverb says, I think I have something of value to offer about the various systems I lived under. The diversity of the various periods I lived in, the various people I worked with, and the various experiences I collected over three quarters of a century. In the sub-title, Decamping communism from the other side of the iron curtain, I tried to compress this message of diverse environments from my past.

Plus, a brief history of the period just preceding my joining the world, are all points of importance that seem easily forgotten these days. Most of my writing is in chronological order, but from time to time I have escaped from that regimen and detoured to a few vignettes from the time in question. I also freely shared my thoughts and opinions about some of the events and developments that took place around me, if I saw them in any way related to my story.

I'm not always politically correct, and more often than not, they diverge from today's prevailing *vox populi* position. I have a problem with the removal of statues and the Orwellian rewriting of history, as shown at the end of Chapter 5. I also object to Senator (and perennial presidential candidate) Bernie Sanders' depiction of socialism with a kind hearth, as mentioned in Chapter 9. He may be a darling of the young masses, a guy who praises Ortega and Castro, and chooses Moscow for his honeymoon venue, but what does that signify? If it walks like a duck, and quacks like a duck, it must be a ... Communist. However, this is not my abbreviated political manifesto, so don't worry, the majority here is just my memories recorded.

I'd be remiss not to mention the last reason for writing. Being locked in place in Miami Dade County, the deadliest of all in Florida since early March, due to the Chinese virus pandemic; What else could one do?

Some of the greatest literary works were produced during pandemics, for example Boccaccio's Decameron. Not that I am trying to put myself on the same level of Boccaccio's, but there are some similarities in activities and events. In the preface to his book, Boccaccio writes that his opus has been done for the comfort and entertainment of his friends during these taxing times.[2]

I too had time on my hands to comfort and entertain my friends. This is all for you all, and I hope it entertains you, and offers you some comfort. On the other hand, Churchill said about his memoirs: "I have consistently urged my friends to abstain from reading it". You can abstain as well, as you have now been forewarned.

Let's start with the day I appeared in this world.

---

1. *Part of the inscription on the Statue of Liberty, in New York harbor*
2. *Decameron was written during the Black death, plague pandemic, mid 14th century, when some 50 to 200 million people, of Asia and Europe, died.*

1

THE HAPPIEST DAY IN THEIR LIFE

• • • ▬

All biographies start with the birth (in the case of autobiographies and memoirs, not necessarily the most accurate reporting segment), and end with the death. Not to break the mold, let us also start with my birth. That may have been The Happiest Day in Their Life, not just for my parents, but for the hundreds of millions of people throughout Europe.

It was D-Day, June 6, 1944, and the BBC's "V" for Victory sign, sent in Morse code, three dots and a dash, their trademark signal, broadcasted to occupied lands during all the war years, woke up the occupied peoples of Europe. That morning it was the lead news story, that the Allied machine had started a long awaited major offensive, to liberate Europe from the German occupation.

But regrettably, D-Day didn't turn out as many had expected. The freedom of Europe was still eleven months, and hundreds of thousands of lives, of both soldiers and civilians, away. So, enthusiasm in the Fischer family was also short-lived. The Allied forces fought for weeks, or months on the Atlantic coast, and another mouth had to be fed in a country ravaged by occupation, civil war and revolution.

Croatia was a German puppet state, established by a gang of emigrants, led by Dr. Ante Pavelić, a Croat from Bosnia. They were originally supported by Mussolini, who even gave them a king, the Duke of Aosta. But Pavelić didn't make much use of him. Pavelić was an enthusiastic follower of Hitler. He declared his racial views already in 1936 with, "The Croat Question"[1.] Once he came to power, he and his police, who supported him with great devotion, began purging the Jews from the society, and sending them to either local concentration camps (17 of them in that small state), or to the concentration camps of the "glorious" Third Reich.

Croatia was fighting liberals, Serbs, Chetniks, trade unionists, and of course, communists. Not having enough troubles at home, Croatia started sending soldiers and marines to faraway places to support the German *Drang nach Osten*, like campaigns in the Azov Sea, Sebastopol, and Stalingrad. They were often incorporated with other units of the Axis' friends or members, like the Italians,

Hungarians and Romanians. Most of the Croatian Stalingrad soldiers, the Croatian 369th Reinforced Infantry Regiment, never came back, and were either killed in action, froze to death, or died on the long marches to various labor camps within USSR, whilst their commander, Colonel Mesić, was executed by the Germans. At the same time, some 91,000 captured soldiers of Field Marshal Friedrich von Paulus' Sixth Army met a similar fate.

So, the family continued to live under the occupation and hoped to see freedom soon. Whilst the WWII started as a Blitzkrieg, and surely was faster and by far more mobile than the WWI, from general Zhukov's victory at Stalingrad, it took almost another two and half years for the Soviet Army to get into Berlin. Nothing moves fast if you have daily air raids, and bombs falling on your head and Fascist troops marching in the streets arresting passersby indiscriminately. This was just another example why patience is a great virtue: By the time the US entered WWII, Britain and Poland were already at war with the Third Reich for 826 days. Czechoslovakia was at war, even longer. Eventually, all of them, at least for a very brief moment, did see liberation and freedom.

> Europeans may have been looking at the period between the Normandy invasion and the eventual defeat of Germany as a period in limbo. Nothing changed for the majority of people in Central Europe.

But in actual terms, the Allied Forces were slogging their way towards Berlin with some 4 million Western allies' soldiers and 6.4 million Soviet soldiers.

All in all, some 133 countries, independent or colonies, had been involved in the war. The large majority was on the side of the Allies, with an estimate that some 300 million soldiers were involved in the fighting. Between the end of the war, as my parents expected it on June 6 1944, and the real end of the war in May 1945, the following few major skirmishes and events happened.

- The Normandy beaches operation itself lasted for a month and a half, with almost half a million military casualties.
- The Battle of Bulge started in December of 1944. Over 100,000 Allied soldiers had been killed, wounded, or taken prisoners.
- Rome fell on June 4, 1944, two days before the "D" Day, but the bloodiest battles in Italy were still to be fought. The Gothic Line was not crossed until the 25th of August 1944, and the Germans didn't surrender in Italy until April 29, 1945. The Italian campaign lasted 20 months.
- In Yugoslavia, major confrontations continued, like nothing had happened on the Western front. Russian troops entered from the east into Yugoslavia, liberated the capital Belgrade, and

stopped at the Syrmia (Srem) front, where a six months long bloody battle developed where the defense of the withdrawing German Army (Group E) from Greece, lay in the balance. That withdrawal was a start of the events that by mid-May of 1945 ended with the Bleiburg massacres.

IN LIGHT OF ALL THIS, with everybody believing that liberation was "just around the corner", waiting was a dangerous game for the many without pure Arian blood, who were living in the occupied territories. Blood purity was not possible to claim for my family. On my father's side, his parents were of Jewish religion and converted to Catholicism just before their wedding in 1898. I would love to say that they saw Jesus. Instead, in the atmosphere of widespread anti-Semitism, they were looking for a better assimilation in various central European societies. They were not the only ones to convert, up to a quarter of a million Jews converted to Christianity in the late 19th century. By the time the Germans and their Croatian collaborators had been chased out of Yugoslavia, 95% of all Jews were either killed or deported to concentration camps. Belgrade, the capital of Yugoslavia, was the first European capital to send a telegram to Hitler, saying that the city was *Judenfrei* (cleared of Jews). Soon afterwards, the German-collaborating state of Nedić' Serbia was declared the second *Judenfrei* European country, following Estonia. Not without reason, the family was worried. The concerns and worries were rooted in the previous fifty years of family travels and decisions, so let me go back a bit to how my father ended up in Zagreb.

---

1. *Pavelić declared four sets of enemies to be fought to extinction: Serbian government, Freemasonry, Jews and Communism. With the exception of the Serbian government, irrelevant to Hitler, the other goals were in sync with the Führer. But there is an irony: Pavelić' movement, Ustaše, grew out of the Croatian Party of Rights (Hrvatska stranka prava), that my grandmother Gizela Rosenthal's uncle, Josip Frank, a Jew himself, headed. I do not believe that the original platform, which he wrote in 1895, included extermination of Jews in concentration camps.*

2

WHY ZAGREB?

My grandfather Hinko, married Gizela Rosenthal, family name later translated into Croatian, as Ružinski, in Zagreb[1]. She was from the nearby town of Daruvar, and a large number of both his and her family lived in Zagreb. Zagreb was part of Croatia, herself part of Habsburg Monarchy. It was very Germanic oriented, and German language was the *lingua franca* of the educated circles. Hinko, originally born in Moravia, came to Zagreb from his studies, with a mechanical engineering degree and a PhD, to find a bride.

Before the first baby was born in 1899, he was already working in Poland. The Family's whirlwind traveling began. Feodora was born in Sosnowice, then my namesake Raoul C. was born in Zurich in 1900. His sister Erna was also born there in 1902, and eventually, my father, Ernst Hinko, saw light in Nüremberg in 1906. In the meantime, grandma's family stayed in Zagreb, as well as a large number of Hinko's family. So the foundation was laid for the faithful and eventual return to Zagreb.

Hinko's brothers were an interesting group of people. One brother was, what we would charitably call today, an adventurer. Traces of him, (after apparently borrowing lots of money), were lost in Brazil, or Argentina. The other brother spent his life as a railway physician. The third, brother Ignaz, also born in Zagreb like his physician brother, ended up being the most famous, although it took some three quarters of a century for his work to be recognized. Being a Jewish man wasn't a big help. He was a builder, architect, contractor, and designer, active in Zagreb. His work encompassed some eighty capital objects. His projects included three hospitals (Klaićeva Childrens', Brestovac and Petrova) and corroboration on a fourth (the Šalata complex). He also built the National bank and Insurance buildings on the main city square, the first cinema and department store (Kastner u. Öhler – NAMA), designed and built few factories (Arko, Bizjak, DTR) and several hotels and summer villas on the Adriatic coast. He was also involved in urban design in Zagreb. He designed an outdoor area between the Croatian National Theatre and the Rector's building of the University of Zagreb.

On my grandmother's side, her brother was the Governor of the Croatian National Bank (a building that Ignaz Fischer built). He was also Honorary Consul of the Kingdom of Norway. His son René Ružinski, the future Honorary Consul of Kingdoms of Denmark and Norway, and later Consul General of Norway, played a major role during and after the war, in my father's private and professional life.

Later, when the time came to make the decision of where to go in order to avoid the Nazi regime, with all the family in Zagreb, it was the obvious choice.

Germany was where they lived for twenty years, and the family really didn't have roots anywhere else; not in Zagreb, not in Ukraine, not in Poland, or Switzerland. My Grandfather moved too much with his various jobs for the family to have a chance to plant roots anywhere.

Years later, when I looked back at the number of places I lived, I saw many similarities. From Zagreb, to Zürich, to London, to Amsterdam, to Hong Kong, to Tokyo, my movement was constant. Eventually, I planted roots in the United States and still live in the home we bought in 1991.

We now spend winters in Florida with Devon, Pennsylvania still being our home.

But first, let's follow the family on their travels, before their return to Zagreb.

1. *Zagreb was the capital of Croatia during the Habsburg period, then of wartime puppet Independent State of Croatia 1941 – 1945, later of Socialist Republic of Croatia as a part of Yugoslavia, and after 1991, Capital of the new Republic of Croatia*

3

GERMAN ENGINEERS BUILD MINES

Everywhere, from Russia to Pennsylvania, Ohio, and Minnesota, it was German engineers who were designing and building coal mines. So, not surprisingly, my grandfather got a job with a Belgian mining company building mines in Donets Basin.

The family moved to Luhansk, (later renamed Voroshilovgrad, and after the collapse of the Soviet Union, renamed Luhansk), in what became part of the family story: Russia.

It took us some time to realize that it was actually Ukraine, but Russians made sure that the distinction was never explained to the foreigners. Until I married my wife Taisa House, who is of Ukrainian ancestry, and my sister married a Ukrainian fellow, we were not that sensitive to such local matters. Russia, Ukraine ... who cares?

Russian propaganda was very successful. Everything was a part of "Big Russia". Every success of the constituent republics was a Russian success. The largest cargo plane in the world, the Antonov A-255 ... Russian.

The largest, allegedly the best mass-produced car line (3.5 Million produced in a 34 years run, with minimal model changes), Zaporozhets ... Russian.

Vladimir Horowitz, David Oistrakh, Isaac Stern and Sviatloslav Richter ... Russian.

Isaak Babel, Joseph Conrad, Ilya Ehrenburg, Nikolai Gogol, and my favorite, Mikhail Bulgakov... all Russian.

Except actually, they were not Russian. Russia quickly distanced itself from Chernobyl. That was Ukrainian problem. For good reason, the Russians also never tried to claim Golda Meir, Simon Wiesenthal, and Nathan Sharansky ... all Ukrainians.

Today, Eastern Ukraine is again occupied by Russian proxies.

Once WWI started, with Gavrilo Princip having been assassinated in Sarajevo, the Archduke Ferdinand, and Sofia, the Duchess of Hohenberg, citizens of the Central Powers (Germany, Austria-Hungary, Ottoman and Bulgaria), were rounded up by the allied forces, all over Europe. The Fischer family was sent to a POW camp in Vologda. Now, they saw the real Russia. Eventually, they were freed through services of the Swedish Red Cross, and via Sweden, ended up in Germany. We, the younger generation, inherited Russian samovars, their souvenirs.

The war and exile actually had a silver lining. The family settled for good, in Germany. My grandfather started running a shipyard, which was a very busy undertaking, because Germany was building for war reparations. All four children received a decent education. With grandfather clearly academically motivated, and acquiring a second PhD in political science sometime, somewhere during their moves, the children knew what was expected from them, nothing less.

Everyone became assimilated in the society. My uncle and my father, while in college, joined the student association, and slowly grew through the ranks. From *Füchsen* through *Burschen* to *Alte Herren* (foxes/kits, fellows, Old Gentlemen), fencing their way up. My uncle hated the shows, and after getting his engineering degree and PhD, eventually left Germany.

On the other hand, my father loved them. My uncle ended up with fencing cuts on his face (*Schmisse*), my father didn't show any, his were on the scalp. This love affair went on until the mid-1930's. Now, the pure aryan blood had to be proven for any officeholder, which my father could not prove. My father was unceremoniously kicked out of the *Burschenverrein* leadership. Luckily for my uncle, he didn't have to go through this shaming process -- he had moved to England by that time.

4

NAZIS TAKING OVER

Armed with a PhD in philology (deals with the structure, historical development, and relationships of a language or languages, as opposed to Linguistics, which is a study of language), my father Ernst Hinko, nicknamed Pelja, began looking for a job at the time of the Great Depression.

Of course, none were available for Doctors of languages. He began as a freelance journalist, and for a period of time held a part-time job in Berliner Tageszeitung, mostly to provide him with press credentials. He turned out to be a very successful journalist and with his Leica camera, a good photographer.

He joined barges and reported on their trips from Lübeck to former German West Africa, delivering construction machinery, built by his father's shipyard, as part of war reparations. That wasn't a happy experience.

Rough weather followed them all the way from the North Sea to the South Atlantic. The tug-boat captains would cut the barges loose in violent weather until the waves subsided, in order to avoid being submerged themselves. Some days later, they would return and collect what was left.

He once reported from The Sahara on a desert trip subsidized by Mercedes Benz. They wisely supplied a mechanic, who turned out to be a godsend and a fairly busy man during most of the adventure. He also reported on travel by trains throughout central Europe, and on smuggling interdictions. In the early thirties, Germany was in the midst of rebuilding, and luxury goods were not high priority items. So, smuggling mostly overland from Denmark and Holland and across the sea from Sweden, was a lucrative business. It was done Chicago style, with submachine guns and armor-plated cars. On a few of the raids, he joined the maritime and railway customs police.

As a *coup de grace*, he flew and reported on the first Lufthansa mail flight in the South Atlantic. The plane was catapulted from a mother-ship in Gambia. It became clear much later that the set-up in Gambia was part of Germany securing communications outposts in the southern Atlantic, in preparation for the coming naval war.

That historic trip in 1933 ended up in the annals of Lufthansa Airlines. He was invited a second time, again a first for a journalist, to join and later write about the Lisbon, Horta (Azores), and then on to a New York flight in 1937.

Both Germans, with Heinkel HA139, and the Americans, with USA Clipper III, were exploring the southern route across the Atlantic, from Horta to New York, because of the harsh conditions for the seaplanes on the northern route.

In 1983 Lufthansa celebrated the fiftieth anniversary of the crossing of the southern Atlantic, and invited all those who took part. Sadly, only the Captain, von Engel and my father were still alive. Captain Blankenburg, of the 1937 Azores crossing also didn't make it. One last time my father interviewed Capt. von Engle, and published the interview in Austria. Later, that same year my father visited me in the United States, and Lufthansa provided a First Class complimentary upgrade.

Lufthansa hydroplane just arrived

HIS JOURNALISTIC CAREER ended abruptly when the Nazi regime declared that anybody involved with newspapers, education, courts and any other public activities, had to prove their pure Arian ancestry for at least two previous generations. Initially, no one in the family saw this as a problem. The family members had already completely assimilated into the German society, and was never told by their parents of that crucial baptism back in the previous century. They believed that none of the anti-Jewish atrocities happening in Germany had anything to do with them.

Aunt Feodora was married to a German medical professor, Fritz Sartorius. Pelja's other sister, Aunt Erna, was married to a landed gentry from Prussia, Mayer-Brügeman, and my father had a Swiss fiancée, Ruthli.

To prove their heritage, they were required to provide the marriage certificate of their parents. They requested the marriage certificate from Sv. Marko, the church in Zagreb where the ceremony was performed in 1898. When the church document arrived in Germany, it showed that the Catholic priest, Father Rajter, added unsolicited remarks under Comment: "of Jewish ancestry".

Apparently, that was his revenge for Jews crucifying Christ. Two marriages, one engagement and two careers were destroyed, in an instant. Three children grew up without their fathers. And the potential transfer to concentration camps and grave danger and death looked to be in their imminent future.

By the end of 1937, the mass murdering of Jews in Germany was in full swing (Kristallnacht had already happened a year before), and anyone who could get exit papers was trying to leave and save their lives. It was clear that remnants of the family had to leave the Third Reich.

Where to?

Zagreb, of course. The grandparents were sent off almost immediately, and the younger generations, (sisters with their children) congregated in Pelja's apartment in

Berlin. Travel arrangements were made and the sisters left before the end of the year. Pelja joined them, with whatever family possessions could be salvaged. Everything was taken to their new home (including samovars!) in the beginning of 1938.

5

FROM ONE DICTATORSHIP, TO ANOTHER, TO A THIRD
(OR, FROM THE FIRE INTO THE FRYING PAN)

On one hand, Yugoslavia was very welcoming. The family instantly received Yugoslav citizenships, based on their Austrian-Hungarian origin.[1] My father received press credentials and his PhD was recognized. However, his unfamiliarity with the language was an obstacle for a journalist. More than ten years passed before he took to the pen again.

On the other hand, my aunt Feodora's credentials were not accepted. Although she'd studied at the University of Hamburg and specialized as a pediatrician in one of the great German universities in Münster, it turned out that that was not recognized by the Zagreb medical guild. Her high school matriculation was also not recognized, and she was forced to retake most of her medical exams. In Croatian!

Incidentally, Feodora was the only one of the siblings who took formal Croatian language lessons. She later lectured at the medical school and published many professional papers. This helped her gain legitimacy and recognition. On the other hand, my father, who later wrote for professional magazines, was "self-taught", and it was noticeable, until the end of his life. All their children, the four of us, were bilingual before we started adding other languages.

Feodora's heydays of work in a University environment were over. She moved in with her son Norman in the small town of Koprivnica, about 80 miles northeast of Zagreb, to serve as a director of a polyclinic.

The decision to move south to Zagreb, away from the Nazi regime, rather than west to England, turned out to be a mistake. In April of 1941, German armies rolled into Yugoslavia, and Croatians established their independent, quisling state. Like Belgium, the operative thinking was that the enemy of my enemy is my friend. Since the birth of the Kingdom of Yugoslavia in 1919, following the First World War, Croatians complained of being suppressed and treated as second-class citizens in their own land. Serbs, like the French in Belgium, controlled the courts, police, military, everything, and now, the opportunity was here.

With the assistance of the Italians and The Germans, Pavelić and his Ustaše organized their own state, and promptly started rounding up Serbs, and of course, Jews.

Didn't everybody do it?

Through some luck and connections, the family in Zagreb was able to live undetected. Their Jewish background was never uncovered, and revealed. They were seen as returning emigrants from Austro-Hungarian times, and nobody questioned their religion. However, it was different in the small town where my aunt was living.

A local doctor is prominent and well exposed, and sooner or later may be scooped up by Nazis. So, my aunt, with her seven-year-old son Norman, joined the partisan movement, and spent the rest of the war as a doctor in various underground hospitals, tending to the wounded.

Grandfather Hinko, retired, out for a stroll

IN THE MEANTIME, my grandfather and his wife, already retired in Germany, stayed in Zagreb. Grandfather died in 1944.

I never met him.

My grandmother lived another twelve years. My father, with his Doctorate of languages in his pocket, was again looking for a job. After stints as a receptionist, in Hotel Bled, Slovenia, and one as a fishmonger, a supplier of exactly 30 cm (12 inches) long river trouts to the Zagreb Hotel Palace, he found his calling making house slippers.

He even got an official certificate as a master slipper and shoemaker. With his cousin René, who I mentioned earlier, and an engineering friend Link, he started a slippers and children's shoe manufacturing facility. René was the commercial manager in charge of distribution, Pelja's main job was securing raw materials like leathers, mostly from adjacent southern areas.

By this time, the Germans no longer occupied the area. Still it was a bit dangerous crossing the frontline, frequently. In 1944 he came back from one of his expeditions with an Opel P4 sedan converted to a truck, a pick-up truck in today's parlance. That car stayed around for another twelve years. I even tried my hand driving it, but that's a different story, for later.

Link was an engineering genius. He kept the factory's ancient machinery working without spare parts, but with a strong will. He spent almost every night taking the cutting, pressing and sewing machines apart, and putting them together so they would be ready for the morning shift. Later in life, Link was sent as a United Nations expert, to Lahore, Pakistan to help build their shoe industry.

The factory evolved from making slippers to becoming the first maker of real children's shoes, not the shrunken variety of adult shoes. Pelja collaborated with an orthopedic surgeon, Dr. Staržek. Together, they fine-tuned the product to fit a child's foot. One of the employees in the company's sales shop was my mother, Ivana Vlahović. She was a Croatian, who spoke good German, learned in trade school.

She was born in Zagreb. Her parents were from nearby Zlatar, and this background sounded like a good cover-up for a Jewish refugee in Nazi territory.

Except, it wasn't.

All four of her brothers were in partisan resistance and two had already been executed by the Germans. Her third brother died in battles in eastern Croatia in 1944, just prior to my birth. Her oldest brother, Josip Vlahović, was declared a National Hero. His name was on a square in Zagreb (Trg Jože Vlahovića). Her fourth brother, Ivica survived the war. After a short stint in the military command of the liberated city of Karlovac, Ivica spent the rest of his career in the military-industrial environment.

Although all four sisters were involved in "Crvena pomoć" the Red Help illegal organization, smuggling supplies to the resistance, all survived the war. My mother's oldest sister became a curator of a museum focused on the history of her oldest brother, Josip. The youngest sister, Marija, nicknamed Beba, is still well, at 93 years of age.

With aunt Beba, in Zagreb, in 2019

IN 1991, following the disintegration of the communist Yugoslavia, one of the first tasks the Croatian nationalists had was to dismantle all monuments and signs of the hated regime. Statues of those who fought the fascist occupation during World War II had to go. Wholesale changes of schools' and streets' names, as well as the square named after my uncle, were enforced.

Mother and father around the time of their wedding in Zagreb

I THOUGHT that that was a Pol Pot type of vandalism. History started repeating itself with Serbians, during the 1991 – 1995 war, destroying some 1,400 catholic churches in Croatia, and the Taliban destroying all cultural objects depicting deities.

Also, now in the States, statues of military and political leaders of the Civil war time are being torn down. Of course, Washington, The Father of the nation, has to go as well. After all, he was a slave owner. The first of his statues was just torn down, this June, in Portland, OR. Followed by Ulysses Grant, Columbus and Cervantes (why him, he was just a writer and himself for five years enslaved?). And in the UK, the mayor of London is taking under advisement removing all signs of British colonialism. Churchill will probably have to go first.

Not much will be left there.

In any case, my father's Vlahović connection surely didn't sound like a great cover during the Nazi occupation.

---

1. *Yugoslavia was one of the territorial successors of the Habsburg Empire, that ceased to exist 1918.*

6

EARLY DAYS BEHIND THE IRON CURTAIN

Now,[1] we have come full circle, and it's my time to reappear in this story. Not long after the end of the war, my parents divorced. Until the age of seven, on weekends I would visit my father, who was then living with my grandmother. Of course, in post war Yugoslavia weekends meant just Sunday. Saturday was a full working and school day.

For a period of time, my father was busy with the factory. However, the Communists confiscated the factory in 1946. The decree was that there were to be no private ownership. Confiscation in the name of the proletariat!

For a period of time he was kept on to manage the factory, but eventually he was forced out. During the old Yugoslavia, until 1991, the factory was still operating under the name "Tvornica dječje obuće Zagreb", but it is gone today.

Eventually, my mother remarried. Under the "three is a crowd" ruling, especially when I got the company of a newly-minted half-sister, I was handed over to my father. He then remarried.

I now had a step-mother. Her name was Vlasta Rytiř, a very proper preppy lady, of Czech origin, from Sarajevo. She was Austrian lyceum educated, and spoke several languages, and also sang, and played piano. I was enrolled in French language classes, piano lessons, and was sent to Sunday morning masses. At that time, I thought it horrible, especially since I had a long and successful experience of having two parents competing. In hindsight, Vlasta was surely wonderful, and raised me to be an acceptable teenager. Except, I missed the Brigitte Bardot movies that all the other kids were allowed to see. By the time I decided to make up for that, Bardot was into animals.

> As a child, I went through two divorces of my parents. I had a father and stepfather, a mother and a stepmother. After my parents divorced, my mother married Zvonko Crnić. He was years her junior (good for her) who was a very nice man. I liked him very much and I would continue to visit him during my occasional return trips to Zagreb, even after my mother passed away.

Zvonko and my mother had two children, my half-sister Ružica (Koka) and my half-brother Želimir (Braco). With Braco I had minimal contact over the years, and eventually none. We kind of went our own way. I thought after his second marriage he became strange. I assume, he thought something similar about me. No harsh words were spoken between us, we just parted. He became a successful mechanical design engineer. After his steel mill in Sisak got destroyed in the war of 1991, he moved back to Zagreb. He divorced and then remarried.

In the later years I started having more and more communication with Koka. I wasn't unhappy in any of the environments that my parents provided, barring the Bardot experience, and I think the idea of a two-parent family is overrated. Three of my best childhood friends, and my future wife, came from single parent homes. None of us has ever shown signs of troubles due to an *"unhappy childhood"*.

That would have been a good excuse in a court of law, although I didn't use it when I was hauled in front of a court (see Chapter 9). I will always take a happy single parent over two fighting ones.

On the subject of *"overrated"*, both my mother and my stepmother Vlasta, later said that kicking my father out, due to his unfaithfulness, was on the balance, a mistake. My mother died whilst she was still young in a traffic accident, in 1968. Then my father passed away of natural causes of old age, in 1993.

Shortly after, both Vlasta and Zvonko passed away of old age. So, after all the fathers, stepfathers mothers and stepmothers, I was an orphan in my late forties.

Father, whilst still working in "his" factory, had to like everyone else, find a second job to support the family. One salary in socialism was just enough to survive. So, he began writing. This time in professional journals. Initially he wrote about leather and shoes, but slowly moved over into plastic. ("Just one word: Plastic," -- remember Dustin Hoffman).

He then began major work on a quadrilingual (French, German, Croatian, English), shoe and leather dictionary. These were pre-computer times, and index cards were all over the apartment. Eventually, by 1960 the dictionary was published.

Father's four-language dictionary

APPROXIMATELY AT THAT TIME, Germany started direct payments as reparations to those injured by their war. The previous reparations were gobbled up by the State, and no Yugoslav citizen saw a cent.

This was a typical case when the State declared itself above the citizens, typical for communist states. This State, which in this particular case didn't even exist at wartime, declared itself as injured, and confiscated German reparations meant for individual actual victims of the Nazi regime. At the same time, the State happily participated in the twenty three billion dollar German war state-to-state reparations as agreed, at the Potsdam conference in 1945.

Compensations were paid based on mostly financial harm, career losses, and income losses. In general, estimates had to be made since most of the records in Germany were destroyed. But, as my father's luck would go, the personnel archives of *Berliner Tageszeitung* newspaper happily survived the total destruction of Berlin. The records showed that my father was just a freelance writer, and consequently couldn't claim a quantifiable salary and job loss. So, he received a minimum monthly payment. But it was still a princely sum in communist Yugoslavia. From the initial proceeds, he acquired a photocopier and started a copying side-business, and paid for my first motorcycle.

Visiting, with my mother and her family. From r. Koka, Zvonko, Braco, mother, self - 1965

WEEKENDS SPENT DOING things with the family was a rule. We spent time driving in the 1936 vintage Opel, doing excursions into the surrounding area. At the young age of ten or eleven, I tried to drive the Opel down a steep hill in the nearby town of Samobor.

I drove the car with no engine running by just releasing the handbrake. General Motors' refusal to go hydraulic until 1938 (GM owned German Opel) saved the day: the car had mechanical brakes and didn't need the engine to be running for me to be able to use the brakes. I did manage to stop it without any physical damage. My father's scolding was a different issue.

Only once did he become physical, but not this time. He only became physical when he caught me lying. I don't know whether I ever lied to him again, but I do remember with embarrassment the time when I got caught. That aside, the custom of family Sunday outings continued into my teenage years and even later, when my father visited from Austria.

A picnic on the Krka river, 1963. From l. self, Makar and his wife Zdravka and Miljenka, my future wife

ZAGREB WAS BLESSED with a large number of small rivers and hot spas not too far away, so there was always somewhere to go for a swim and BBQ. My father had a car, my cousin Norman had a car, I had a motorbike, and my future best man, Stanko had an antique Fiat 500 convertible, so everybody and our respective girlfriends would gather during these summer outings.

After leaving the factory, father changed jobs several times. He first worked at an export-import company. These were a Communist invention, buffers to separate innocent and naïve domestic buyers, from aggressive and corrupt capitalist sellers.

At one point, my father and Vlasta divorced, and we moved into his Grandmama's place, which for him, was a full circle. We now lived in my aunt's and my cousin Norman's home. It was a big place, well over two thousand square feet for four of us, not to mention the dog and a fish tank. With a little bit of give and a little bit of take, we survived quite well in the close quarters.

This was the home where my father left for Austria and I went to college, and eventually to an apartment that my aunt found for me. From Grandmama's place, her son Norman and his wife Verica left initially for India, and then on to Switzerland. At the end of the day, from the initial crowd, my aunt was left alone in that big house.

Working for the Export-Import company afforded my father opportunities for his first post-war business trip to the West. On his return, I saw my first banana but that disappeared before I had a chance to try it. Later I rationalized that it didn't really look appealing to me.

From the first Ex-Im business Centralcommerce, he moved to the second one, Feronia. After that, he became commercial director of a shoe distribution chain, Obuća.

Next was a marketing job with a company producing and distributing Yugoslav movies called Globus Film. After addressing a letter to a customer in East Berlin as "East Germany", he was fired.

Our communist friends in the German Democratic Republic didn't like that, and filed an official complaint. They were the democratic version of Germany, not just an eastern province of the successful West Germany. So, after twenty-five years calling Yugoslavia home, he left for Austria.

In Graz he was the commercial director of another shoe distribution chain for a period of time, named Stieffelkönig. Later he started his own trading company.

I however, stayed behind. Since I was never a problem in school and managed to get enrolled in University in 1962 based on my academic scores, my father didn't see a problem leaving me to my own devices. A point to remember, whilst students in the US almost regularly leave, or try to leave their nest when looking for colleges, the same is more an exception than a rule in Europe.

I enrolled into the School of Electrical Engineering, not because this was my lifelong dream, but because my first choice, the Mechanical Engineering School had a shortened summer break by a month! That seriously interfered with my summer plans to take a motorbike tour of Italy. But all's well that ends well.

While definitely not a great student, I had many and varied interests. Mostly playing cards, running around on my bike and dabbing into many different sports, for very short times. Kayaking, fencing, ice-skating and judo. Squash, racquetball and golf came later. The only ones that I enthusiastically continued were tennis and skiing. I also enjoyed sailing, even when it was raining and hard blowing, but I never considered it a sport. For a couple of summers I got a job with Hertz, ferrying cars.

I tried my hand at writing, and got one interview published with the head of the Styria, the governor of Steiermark, Austria. The rest of my career in the student newsletter called the Studentski list, was unremarkable.

Hard at work: Editorial office of Studentski list

For some reason, in 1963 I got selected to join a delegation of Croatian students to visit with Serbian students in Belgrade. It is hard to remember what was discussed, but obviously nothing controversial, because we didn't get kicked out of college upon our return. We probably discussed something about better cooperation between our universities and of course, world peace.

With a student delegation in Belgrade. Avala, Zdenka and self, third and fourth from left

One of the delegation members was Zdenka Delalić, whom I lost track of, but met again twenty eight years later, in Philadelphia. She became a Temple

University professor, and later made a name for herself in the nanotechnology field. She also played a very active role as a leader of the local Alumni Chapter of The University of Zagreb, during the War in Croatia, 1991 -1995. She was one of those highly intellectual and successful ladies, playing games with her age. When we met again in the United States at a group gathering, she refused to admit knowing me, or that we were colleagues in college. That would have dated her. She was actually one year my senior. Since nobody paid any attention to the age issue, she eventually got over it.

My father remarried in Austria, and I visited him regularly and spent every Christmas in Graz. In the early eighties, he started contributing again in Austrian newspapers on subjects of general interest. He wrote stories about,

- Rebuilding Skopje, the capital of Macedonia, following the earthquake.
- The 356 churches in Ohrid, a town on a lake in Macedonia.
- About small towns in Slovenia, on the Adriatic Coast.
- Vacationing in Portugal.
- Train traveling through Europe and the earlier mentioned anniversary interview with the Captain of his first Atlantic flight.

He and his wife built a nice house in the suburbs of Graz, with a fair-sized garden, and it was a pleasure to come to visit and escape the bustle of a busy city. Initially, it would be me and my wife, and later my friends joined too. Graz was the shopping place for luxury-goods starved Yugoslavs, and the great excitement was smuggling the acquisitions back to avoid customs duties.

With studying done and traveling done, there were no more excuses to delay growing up.

It was time to get serious.

But first, another rare picture of the family: all four siblings together, in Zagreb, 1966. Uncle Raoul C. visiting from London, and Erna and Pelja coming from Graz. The last time they were all together must have been in late fifties, also in Zagreb.

From left: Raoul C., aunt Feodora, aunt Erna, my father

---

1. *The expression "Iron Curtain" was in use for some time, incl. in a 1945 message by Yugoslav imprisoned Prime minister Vladko Maček, in a letter, from his house arrest to New York Time's Sulzberger. The phrase got wide usage after Churchill's speech in Fulton, talking about the curtain falling down from Baltic to the Adriatic Sea. And the dawn of theCold War.*

7

THE FIRST EXPOSURE TO A REAL JOB

By 1968 at age of 24, I managed to get my engineering and master's degree and finish my military service. I was married and had my first job. I was doing all that was expected, from a good son.

My military service picture

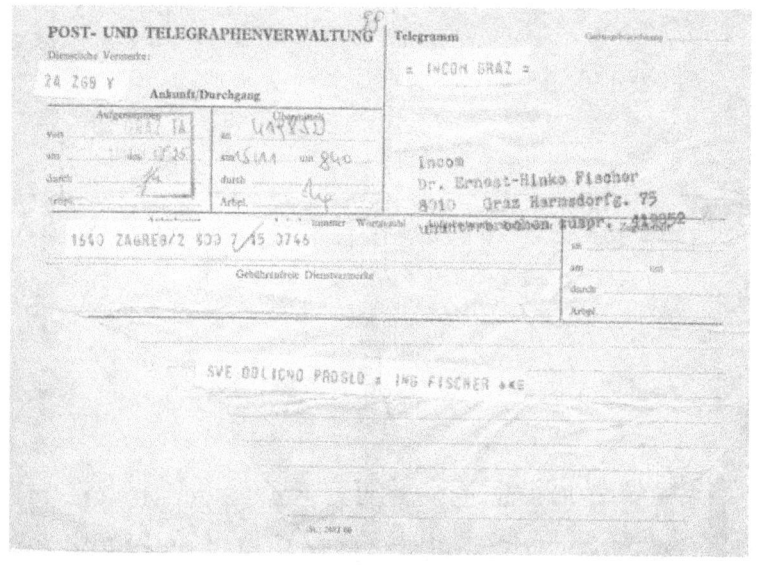

The telegram I sent to my father advising him that I graduated (not a big production like in the States)

Military service in Yugoslavia was obligatory for men. Twelve months for college educated, eighteen months for those without a degree and twenty-four months if they served in the Navy. I served my twelve months in a place some 150 miles east of my home, in an engineering unit. I was trained and exposed to operating and maintaining trucks (original duce-and-a-half), CAT earthmoving equipment, tug boats, pontoon transports (at 2.3mpg, we were not running them a lot), and anything else that moved.

I served during the ouster of the Minister of The Interior, Aleksandar Ranković (as opposed to the similarly named American department, his ministry did not run the parks and recreation, but the secret police. He got caught spying on the President – didn't we hear a similar story recently?).

The next morning after Aleksandar Ranković was ousted, the political class officers were at a loss with the developments, like the rest of the population. So, our class was cancelled with a warning not to form any opinions, since the opinions would be delivered later in the day. It was a power struggle between the (secret) police and the Army that supported Tito.

The Army won.

A bit about the languages: As a child, I grew up bilingual. My mother spoke to my father mostly in German. Visiting grandma was also a German speaking affair, so the German language came easily. I am glad that I was pushed as a child into French, and took up lessons again later. My French knowledge peaked around the age of 20, and then it was downhill from there. On the occasional trip to France, I managed to survive.

English I took at school. In the last year, a friend of mine and I did English conversations with Miss

Corrin, a visiting English student. Another big help was that Yugoslavia did not dub foreign movies. They showed movies with the original language and subtitles. It was a great way to pick up a basic understanding of a few languages, including Italian, which I never really studied, but acquired a working knowledge of. And most importantly, in my teenage years was Anglo-Saxon pop music.

One would not always acquire the richest and most sophisticated vocabulary from this source, some of it not even necessarily usable in mixed company. Like Tom Lehrer's lyrics in Poisoning Pigeons in the Park, or Masochist Tango.

Once in Japan, I managed to get to a survival level of Japanese, and recently started studying Spanish, a must in Miami, the ex-territorial capital of Cuba. The investment in the English language paid well from day one of my professional life, as well as my social life, since English was either the official language, or *lingua franca*.

My INITIAL INTENTION was not to even look for a job in Yugoslavia. I sent my resume to several companies in Western Europe, and even before graduating, got a job offer from English Electric Ltd. (later ICL) in Britain. But the salary was abysmal at 105 Pounds (some $260) a month.

My uncle Raoul, who was living in the London suburbs at that time, said that if I stayed with him, I may be able to survive for several months until the next salary review.

Britain wasn't in great economic shape, and was actually heading into even worse territory[1]. Not the Eldorado I was looking for.

Then a friend, Darko Iveković, who was working with IBM at the time, started working on me. He used all the sentimental arguments he could muster, about leaving your home, friends and other heartbreaking details, and got me to apply for a job with IBM in Zagreb, for a princely sum of $115 per month (144,500 dinars).

What one does for friends.

The job was not in engineering, but in computer software, working for the IBM department of a Slovene firm. I have always regarded the first four years as a very useful apprenticeship period. All the novices were sent to Austria for initial training in data processing. Then we did a stint on the job. Later some of us were sent to Sindelfingen, the German IBM Headquaters, for system analysis and coding training. In Sindelfingen I managed to see on a color TV, Armstrong and Aldrin land on the moon in July of 1969.

Then, there was another stint at the training facilities in the United Kingdom, and I was ready to be unleashed onto the unsuspecting data processing users of Yugoslavia. IBM was a great company, but the prospects of promotions in the medium-term future were bleak. It was a relatively young organization. My boss and my boss' boss were only a few years older than I was, and there was no way I would wait for their retirement before advancing.

I tried to apply for the head of computer maintenance. My engineering degree made me more qualified than the incumbent, but I was told to forget it. The incumbent was the secretary of the communist party cell and a reserve captain of the Yugoslav army.

Bad idea!

So, I moved from system engineering to marketing and received the most beautiful geographic area to look after, Dalmatia, on the Adriatic coast. The company even chipped in for a car. My colleagues and I managed to sell some major computer systems in Split, Metković and Dubrovnik.

We sold computer systems to shipyards, banks, and trading companies. Later, I will mention my childhood friend Vilko Koren again, but here he fits well into the story. At about the same time Vilko, the petroleum engineer, had enough with drilling for oil, and applied to join IBM. One of prerequisites was a working command of English, which he didn't bring with him from highschool. So, he joined me on one of my regular trips down the coast, and got two weeks of total immersion in English. He got the job, but probably hated the trip. For entertainment and more importantly, some additional income, I joined the faculty of Varaždin Data Processing College. I liked the teaching environment, but as a career, this was not an option.

> On the social scene, besides our own friends, we inherited friends of my cousin Norman once he left for the UK, India and eventually, Switzerland. Darko's (who I mentioned previously) wife Vida was from the original Norman circle, and we spent a lot of time together. Both in Zagreb, then skiing in Slovenia, Italy and Austria, and at their place on the Adriatic coast on the island of Vrnik. We stayed in contact with Vida after our departure for the Far East and the United States, until her demise a few years ago.
>
> Darko stayed with IBM. He was one of the young managers who I didn't want to wait for his retirement. Once he and Vida divorced, I didn't see him for decades, until recently. As if there never was a time gap of many years, we enjoyed each other's company immensely.
>
> Then, there was Makar, a TV and movie director. I think he started as Norman's poker-playing friend,

and later his best man. We saw a lot of him, until we departed Yugoslavia.

There was also Predrag Keros, Norman's colleague, and his wife Jadranka. She was a classmate and a namesake of my wife, and they would visit occasionally when we lived on Zvonimirova Street. Our apartment in Zvonimirova became the gathering place for all of our friends. Some were regulars, like Vilko who would come every Tuesday for spaghetti carbonara. Alka, my former buddy from the last two years of college, became a regular once she divorced her husband. Viktor Ivanović, my best man, and Malina and Fred were also quite frequent visitors.

In subsequent years, on my visits to Zagreb, I would go on Sundays to see Predrag. He was "holding court" in a restaurant near the Cathedral, and everybody who wanted to see him, knew just where to find him.

From right: Vanča, Zdravka, Jadranka Keros, Makar and self, dinner in Zvonimirova

Occasionally, Osman, one of Norman's original friends, who we continued to see from time to time, would also join in. Darko and Makar are well and still living. Osman and Predrag have passed away by now. But here I am jumping ahead a few years. So, let's continue with the professional side.

---

1. *A few years later, with all the strikes, coal miners and transportation, there was a lack of everything in the UK. At that time (1974/1975), I was commuting between Amsterdam and London, and would bring fresh bread and sugar to my uncle. The bread he accepted, at the sugar he would frown. He didn't want me to do it again -- he would suffer with the rest of his countrymen. Stiff upper lip and all that stuff.*

8

LOOKING AT NEW OPPORTUNITIES

Back to career progressions. After four years at IBM an opening came up. One day the director of the office, Franjo Faber, threw a copy of *Computerworld*, a British published trade weekly on my desk. He said, "Look at that, Sperry Univac is trying to expand into the market".

By that time IBM had the largest computer market share. Me and the marketing director, Zdravko Mršić of course ridiculed that idea and made appropriate noises. Then we rushed over to the Xerox machine and ran off two copies of the ad. The proverbial ink wasn't even dry yet, and two letters went out.

Univac, a division of Sperry Corporation[1], already had existing systems installed. The Željezara Sisak, The Federal Accounting office, Borovo, and Energoprojekt. Following the success of securing a large mainframe contract with the University of Zagreb, Univac decided to build a team in Yugoslavia, and was looking for people with a marketing background. Interviews were set up, and in short with my two 100% IBM Club marketing rewards, I got the marketing job.

I was based in Zürich, but never got a residency there. I was the youngest general manager, and the youngest company vice president, until I wasn't the youngest anything anymore.

I retired in 1993[2]. The longer version is a bit more complicated, and takes us through three continents and many countries in my journey to retirement.

The Swiss residency restrictions made it better for me to move from Zurich to London, where I became a permanent resident and eventually even became a State pensioner. In the ensuing ten years, I did not spend much time in England. I continued to work for the Swiss corporation. I worked in Amsterdam, Yugoslavia, and eventually in the British Crown Colony, Hong Kong. It gave me a chance to spend time with my uncle, Raoul C.

Out of all the family members, I think we had the most in common. Unlike others, we both loved sailing, and did some sailing together on the English Channel and in Solent. As a teenager, I visited him in England in 1961, got my first chance to drive his Jaguar, something every kid would remember, and I also got a chance to see my first nuclear power plant, in Bradwell.

Sexy, right?

At that time Raoul was the managing director of Head Wrighston, a company that designed and built cooling systems for nuclear reactors. Not surprisingly, when I applied for the UK entry visa, he got a visit from MI6, inquiring about the request from a communist country citizen. After sharing all their atomic secrets with the Russians via the Cambridge Five, nothing was left to disclose anymore so they eventually decided to close the barn doors.

But my visa was approved. Later, they even granted me a permanent residency. Raoul, initially a mechanical engineer, changed his interests to petroleum engineering, and then to nuclear engineering. Once he retired at the early age of 62, his retirement agreement prevented him from continuing in the nuclear arena, and he went back into petroleum and specifically, drill-bits and cooling mud. That's what he was doing when I came back to the UK in 1973.

A nice anecdote from the time of my visit to the Bradwell nuclear site.

Uranium was not easily assessable (possibly translated into expensive), the driver employed by the power plant decided to get away with two rods of U235. Not being the brightest kid on the block, he thought he would become rich and famous selling them on the open market. MI5 (thinking it was the doing of a foreign power), MI6 (thinking it was an act of domestic terrorism), and Scotland Yard, joined in the hunt. But it was the local bobby who noticed a truck with a faulty rear tail light, and stopped it. I assume, by that time, the car was already glowing and didn't need a tail light. The power plant got the rods back in almost original shape, half-life time being 704 million years.

IN THE MEANTIME, my marriage of seven years was going slowly south. My job involved lots of traveling. My wife Miljenka, an architect after working for several years in a design bureau, decided to go back to studying urban planning and was working on her master's degree. We drifted apart and eventually divorced in 1975.

> Miljenka and I were high school sweethearts from junior year. Both of us loved to travel, and did so with great frequency, together and separately. All our friends were common friends from our childhood. We had many common interests, art and architecture were two. We spent a lot of time together and by the time of our wedding, we had known each other for eight years.
>
> Some high school loves survive, others don't. After seven years of marriage, we split. Our friends split

along the "his fault/her fault" line. I ended up with Vilko, my friend since grade school. Miljenka walked away with some others, who surprisingly, I never saw again.

With Vilko I went from grade school through high school. We studied different subjects in college. He studied petroleum engineering, while I was studying electrical engineering. We were reunited at IBM, where he remained until his retirement. He was the best man at my wedding. I was his.

He lost his wife to a traffic accident and stayed a single father to his daughter Ana. Today, Ana is a grown-up lady with a son named Oskar. While still in Hong Kong, Vilko and his new wife Marija visited us in Hong Kong and later, in the States. The last couple of years, Tess and I, Vilko and his wife Marija, spent summers traveling neighboring countries in Europe, until the Chinese pandemic started and everybody got locked up in their respective abodes.

Getting on the Univac team took a bit of pushing. It turned out that the "big" expansion plan approved by the Sperry Univac corporate headquarters provided for hiring only one marketing person. Zdravko, my senior at IBM already a marketing manager with more experience, was a shoe-in. It was now up to me to explain to the company representative Fred Davies, why it would be in his best interest to hire me as well.

He eventually did, and this turned out to have been in his best interest. When the opportunity for his promotion came, he was able to point out that he had already secured a successor. In 1975 when Fred got a new job running COMECON which served Eastern European countries based in Vienna Austria, I came from Amsterdam and stepped into his shoes. Simultaneously, I was made a *prokurist*[3] of the swiss company USAG (Univac Services AG).

> Over thirty years, Fred and I, and our wives, Malina and Jadranka, became best friends. Fred was a very interesting person who was great to be with and with whom I could discuss a range of topics. Originally from Bristol Wales, and a product of the British public-school system, Fred was a trained physicist, with a PhD from ETH in Switzerland. He was fluent in German and French, and had seen the world.
>
> Initially, Fred was my boss for two years. After a period of time when I was in Asia, he became my manager again. But after a short period of time, he left the company and joined Castolin Euctectic, a US privately held Corporation, to run their European operations, out of Lausanne Switzerland.
>
> Apparently, Fred wasn't happy with the set-up. Shortly before he left, I was approached by the US HQ of Castolin, to run their worldwide marketing operation.

Fred's reaction, "Did they offer you the use of the private jet? Don't believe it! They did that to me too, it's just a teaser. It takes more time to fill the request forms than the actual flying time." In any case, I didn't move to Flushing, NY.

Shortly after, Fred started his own banking software company, which he built into a very successful business. Most of his market was in Switzerland and Germany, so he headquartered his business in Zürich, and commuted every weekend back to London, where his home and Malina were. This did wonders to his accumulated Swiss Air mileage. We continued to see them in Switzerland and the UK, and later in the US. Malina was our Maid of Honor. We spent almost every summer visiting a different European country, until eventually, Jadranka and then Fred died of cancer in very short order.

My job running the Yugoslav operation started with a big bang. That was the sound of doors closing on all imports. Yugoslavia, thanks to the economic expertise and endless wisdom of the leaders, all based on Marxist-Leninist philosophy, eventually managed to run out of foreign currency, and of sources for additional foreign loans. Or, as Margaret Thatcher said, they run out of other peoples' money.

At approximately $20 billion in debt (a State secret the International Herald Tribune was regularly writing about), the West said NO to any more loans. And the East, The Soviet Union and its satellites, never offered anything beyond solidarity slogans, good wishes and non-convertible rubles. Not something one could use to procure American data processing systems. So my job, rather than trying my great new ideas, starting new marketing campaigns and entering new fields, focused on cost cutting and endless discussions with the banks for securing at least some foreign currency.

That was the time of post-oil shock, when INA, the largest oil company and largest corporation in Yugoslavia, was urgently in need of more computer power and more ability to search for oil, both in the Adriatic Sea and inland, in eastern Croatia. It was also the first time I visited the USA. Whilst trying to sell a new computer to INA, I went with a group of their experts to Houston, the oil HQ of America.

We were shopping for seismic exploration software. In a changed role, I was the buyer, well not really, but I was leading a group of buyers. I loved the wining and dining that we were exposed to.

I was impressed with all that I saw. The rental car was at least twenty-two feet long, the gas stations wouldn't take my money, but rather preferred InterContinental's plastic VIP card. Booze in the bars had to come with a steak, which was later thrown away, and after a couple of drinks, a whole cow was wasted. For a day we went on a gambling river paddle boat, where they only served near beer. There was no way to jump the ship. We started appreciating the steaks with booze in Houston.

I got to stay in The Plaza Hotel in New York, a place I saw back home on the silver screen, in "North by Northwest". I saw the Guggenheim museum, and went to Broadway musicals, Jesus Christ Superstar and Cabaret. My initial impression of America was that it was definitely a place to return to. Eventually, I did.

That was a lot of fun, but on the professional side we managed to secure the required software and support for the seismic application from a Houston outfit Geocom, and that was a prerequisite for a large, multiprocessor hardware deal.

Due to the harsh economic situation, the focus of all marketing activities had to be where the money was, oil corporations, export companies generating foreign currency, the police and military.

Slowly business picked up and we signed up a few key accounts, primarily INA Oil Corp., Energoinvest in Sarajevo, an investment and engineering company working mostly overseas, several state police accounts, banks, and a Joint Venture with the Department for Military Procurements, computerizing a military plane builder, and two other manufacturing sites.

The expansion, with large contracts, caused a big problem due to the lack of qualified support staff. Yugoslavia had its own specific economic problems, but the rest of Europe was booming, led by Germany. In the early seventies, schools hadn't yet adapted to the new computer age. Almost all of the software experts were self-taught college graduates in fields as varied as philosophy, math, physics, and engineering. But the supply was limited, and all I could offer were assignments in not very attractive places, behind the Iron Curtain.

So, quite often some strange characters got attracted. I never complained about their performance, but I had to live with their occasional strange behavior. I often had to pull the hot iron out of the fire, since their free views would occasionally conflict with the law and order of a Yugoslav state.

For instance, one of the hardware experts who came from Japan, got involved in a traffic accident and claimed to be part of the Vojvodina police. True, he was maintaining computer systems there, but was not their undercover agent, which the chief of police explained to me in detail in a late-night phone call. Things get lost in translation, especially with Japanese.

Another conversation with the police included one of our Austrian accountants. His landlord called the police because Dietrich was annoyed that the landlord wouldn't allow him to keep his horse in the garage, and brought the horse into his apartment. While removing the horse, the police found a gun. This was something a normal person, with an IQ over twenty five, wouldn't try to smuggle into a Communist country.

The lucky guy was allowed to drive back to Austria, without the gun or his wife, who stayed behind. She was my secretary. I needed a trilingual secretary, so we imported one from Austria. She began keeping a German Shepard under her desk, since with her husband and horse gone, the animal felt sad and lonely.

Then there was also a very short lived Belgrade branch manager. He was a Swiss guy who decided to get a pork roast for the New Year's celebration, and started *ab ovo*, from the very beginning. He bought a live piglet and was walking it down the streets of Krugujevac, Serbia, on a string wrapped around its hind leg.

Some of the other stories are probably not printable, but there was another bright one. Our family of expatriates expanded when one of the British support guys married President Tito's niece.

In addition to expanding the customer base, I also had to look after the existing contracts. The largest one I inherited (that Fred Davies was instrumental in selling), was SRCE -- the University Data Center for the combined University of Zagreb, my Alma Mater.

The management team of SRCE almost entirely consisted of my former professors, starting with Prof. Turk, the technical director. He was my dissertation mentor seven years prior.

Later, I had to deal with Prof. Stefanini, which presented a new issue. He was the father of my school friend Tamara. He only saw me as that kid who was his daughter's friend (in college, I took none of his courses) until I took over for the Yugoslav operation. Against that background I had to establish myself as a person, irrespective of my background as a student of these demi-gods, solely in control of the operations and support of their enterprise, as well as an equal business partner.

Like every large project, this one had its share of problems, and eventually it was up to my organization to provide the proper support. We all got along well and I appreciated those interesting times.

On the lighter side: When we installed the interim system, an UNIVAC 1106, that multimillion dollar computer system would be crashing in irregular periods, without any reasonable explanation. Until it was discovered that each time a tram would pass by the building, the crash would occur. The grounding of the system was in a manhole underneath the tracks, and contacts were shaken by the tram's passing. The original site in Savska was abandoned and new system was installed in a dedicated computer center.

AFTER THREE YEARS at the Yugoslav job, I was offered a new bigger one far away. But not before I managed to run into a few legal and political problems. Regrettably, the above newly established relationship with the President didn't help.

---

1. *My entire career, bar four years, I spent with Sperry Corporation (and its successor) and in this text various names of the same entity appear. Hence the need for clarification. Sperry Corp. was a US corporation, operating worldwide. It was a conglomerate of series of mostly hi-tech divisions. Sperry Univac (computer systems) represented some 50% of total business. After 1986, following the merger with Burroughs Ltd., all other divisions but Sperry Univac were sold off, and the company was (and is today) operating under the name Unisys.*
2. *All in all, I worked for only two employers in my whole career. Compared to my father, who worked, for as far as I could determine, more than ten. We were different.*
3. *A holder of the company power of attorney, a first for a Swiss company from a communist country – or so they told me when I had to register my signature with the Zürich Canton court.*

9

PUBLIC ENEMY

As a Yugoslav subject running a foreign company, often telling banks and companies some unwelcomed truths, as well as controlling the payments and expenses of workers' enterprises, I began to be perceived as an enemy. I stepped on too many toes. It was tolerable when foreigners were doing that, but a local boy?

So, one day in 1978, two inspectors appeared in the office, almost like walking off the silver screen: Grey eyes, grey suits, thick rubber soles. One of them was I. Dimitrović, the other never bothered to introduce himself. They proceeded to begin interviewing everybody who would, or would not, have any information, but they never disclosed on what. Eventually, the Corporation and I were served indictments accusing us of attempting to undermine the Yugoslav Self-Management system.

Nothing less.

In a Communist country, that's somewhere on par with treason.

Apparently, it was all initiated by an anonymous call from a Workers Council member. They seriously disliked the financial controls I had introduced, due to a total ban on imports. So, our business was down to providing hardware services and software consultancy. The good old times, when the sales commissions had been used for various activities dear to the Workers Council, were gone. But in a system where it was expected that everybody is provided for, irrespective of financial situation of the company, or the state for that matter, this wasn't well accepted.

From accusations of not allowing free spending, to accusations of undermining the system, there was just one short step. On some level, in a parallel world with more flexible or esoteric rules, or where spending and earning are not interconnected, they were probably right. Yes, I did disagree with several Workers Council decisions. Yes, I did not approve salary increases and bonuses at the time of zero economic activity. Yes, I insisted on postponing several expensive overseas trainings, and yes, I introduced limits on inventories. The one step that a manager would normally do, I didn't take: Workforce level adjustment (euphemism for firing). Mostly because one couldn't be fired in Yugoslavia, where workers owned the businesses, or so they were led to believe.

We were hauled in front of a new type of court, specifically established to protect the recently passed Self-Management laws. This being 1978, and Yugoslavia in a more relaxed communist system phase, unlike the Soviet Union of the Brezhnev time, permitted US headquarters and my Swiss corporation to bring in foreign lawyers. I had a local attorney. The good old times of reading the indictment in the local tongue were still used, irrespective of the accused's ability to understand it. But interpreters were allowed.

So, the lawyers asked for a translation of the proceedings. That caused a problem because this court was never meant to be involved in international disputes, (their charge was to defend against enemies from within), and consequently didn't have any budget for interpreters. Nor did the robbed gentlemen[1] speak any foreign languages.

Eager to conclude the case as soon as possible, the judge decided that I, the first accused, should translate the proceeding for the benefit of the court and the foreign lawyers. Since the Swiss lawyer confessed to knowledge of only German, (despite speaking, like most Swiss, also French, Italian and English, possibly even Rhaeto-romanic), it took almost the whole first day translating formalities from Croatian into German and English, and then, back from German and English into Croatian. One would almost find this a farce, if one could forget that at the end of the day, the court had every intention to stick me into a prison, for undermining the Communist system.

My attorney requested court and/or the judges' exemption, based on some obscure legal argument. The US lawyer stated, that since the Court has involved an American corporation, that this looks to him to be an international commercial dispute, and consequently should be handled through an arbitration. The Swiss lawyer helpfully suggested moving the venue to Genève, of course.

Eventually, the proceedings were interrupted, the judge took the objections under consideration, and the court decided to call it a day. The Judge probably wanted to seek guidance from those higher up. The inspectors' visits continued, their gray complexion never changed. More witnesses were deposed, and more court sessions were held. By the time I left Yugoslavia, the Kafkian case was proceeding, however my passport was never confiscated[2].

After four years, the case was closed. I was advised by my lawyer of the Court decision.

IN 1982, the court eventually gave in, and threw the case out. I assume because they lost their only interpreter -- by then, I was in Asia.

But before we go there, a little bit more about the Communist system of my homeland. Not necessarily because I was enamoured with it, but more because I am afraid that communism is rising its ugly head again with the younger generations who never either experienced it, or lived at the time when half of Europe was enslaved.

Initially, after the revolution of 1917, there was a stream of American intellectuals returning from the Soviet Union and trying often successfully, to present to the western world the great benefits of the workers' paradise. Lenin called them useful idiots. The extreme situation came at the time of the Ukrainian famine (Holodomor -- 1932-1934), where some 6 million people, thanks to Stalin's new agricultural policies, starved to death.

At the same time journalists like W. Duranty of The New York Times claimed that the famine in the Ukraine was "malignant propaganda", and it was the invention of enemies to the people. He and The New York Times got a Pulitzer prize for reporting on the subject. And they weren't the only ones. Other prominent subjects who fell for the Big Soviet Lie, include Bernard Shaw and H. G. Wells, who after returning from the "Potemkin" show prepared especially for them, denied that there was any famine in Ukraine.

It is not surprising that today, where history is being pushed out of schools' curriculum, that more and more people are prepared to believe in the second coming of Socialism. They are helped by people like Oliver Stone, determined to rewrite post-WWII history. His attack on Churchill's speech in Fulton, Missouri[3] as being full of lies about the Soviet Union is a beauty: Churchill talked about an iron curtain that fell from the Baltic Sea to Trieste, with Soviet tanks in the streets of almost all Eastern European capitals, but Yugoslavia's. Meantime Stone claims that the Soviets didn't have one aggressive bone in their body. We stopped teaching history, and we will pay for it.

1. *Yugoslav courts at that time had a presiding judge, in my case judge Vulesija, and two advising judges (judge-juror), who were not required to be trained lawyers. They were a mere decoration, with the presiding judge running the show*
2. *This would normally be standard procedure and step one, but as mentioned earlier, this court was not set up for any kind of international business, and the judge mismanaged that.*
3. *The Untold Story of the United States, Season 4*

10

CONTROLLING THE MASSES

In the meantime, I got together with my (to be) second wife Jadranka, and we got married in 1977. Further on, I will devote more space to her, but let's look more at the communism I left behind. My experience with the Yugoslav legal system was nothing compared to Jadranka's father.

The time span was thirty years, and some things did change. For the cardinal sin of trying to leave the Workers' Paradise (running across the border) in 1948, he was sentenced to death.

That's how much the system loved its citizens. Or, as Walter Ulbricht, the Chairman of the Communist party of East Germany said, "These people do not deserve this government." He then unleashed tanks on them.

Jadranka's father's death sentence was commuted to life, and eventually, he was released after eight years, minus his civil rights. From the day the Communists took over, and people realized what the new system was all about, everybody was trying to run to the West. It all started with mass executions of real and imagined enemies, not just people involved with Nazis or the puppet state, but civilians, and intellectuals. In Dubrovnik, most of the *intelligencia* who survived the Italian occupation, and the subsequent, brief German one, got executed on the Daksa Island in 1944.

In the First Chapter I was writing about the Soviet's UF-3 Army and the German Army Group E fighting in 1944 on the Syrmia front. The Germans were trying to secure their back, for withdrawal to the West. The idea was not only to bring as much of the army home as possible, but to secure withdrawal of civilians as well.

From the beginning of the 1900's, Yugoslavia had a large population of Germans in the Vojvodina and Bosnia region. Some were collaborating with the German occupation army, but many did not. However, all were at risk like all the other ethnic Germans in the now liberated places. In 1930, some 30 million Germans lived outside the Reich, some 10 million of them in Europe, mostly in Czechoslovakia, Poland, The Baltics, Ukraine, Romania and Yugoslavia. So, they, and many other civilians started following the German Army's withdrawal west.

The news of score-settling in liberated territories by the Partisans, caused many to try to reach the Allied western front. Besides the Folksdojčers (as these Germans were called), and various Yugoslav civilians of all ages, there were also parts of the regular, conscript, Croatian army (Domobrani), and formerly collaborating military forces and groups, like Chetniks and Ustasha, who were losing the war with the Yugoslav partisans.

Once this colorful band reached the Allied forces at the Austrian border, they were at the mercy of the future UK Prime Minister, Harold MacMillan,[1] They were handed over to the partisans in Bleiburg, on 15th of May 1945. No differentiation was made based on civilian status, sex, age or political orientation. Some seventy to eighty thousand people were executed, the rest were sent to eastern Yugoslavia concentration camps.

Not without reason, it was called the Death march. The killings, starvation and exhaustion decimated the columns of people walking some 600 miles in the heat of the summer. Those who survived had horrible stories to tell. I personally knew three people who did it. Two were underage brothers, the third was a student in the Croatian military academy. (Lujo Lazić). He even wrote a book, "Stations of the Cross" (Križni put), about his experience. Of course, the book couldn't be published in Croatia, until after the fall of communism.

CONTROLLING THE MASSES 77

Once the new system was established, then came the general expropriation of property. Shops, factories, real-estate, and bank accounts. Then came lagers, for the "politicals", like the Goli otok remote island camp. Then the general firing of most of the managers who were not party members. Their replacements' qualifications for the jobs were their party memberships, not the knowledge of the business.

Not surprisingly, a country coming out of four years of war had no chance to recover. Tito, the supreme leader, rejected the Marshall plan, like all the other Soviet satellites, and the economic gap between the East and the West became insurmountable.

Decent jobs were rare, and at the same time, workforce mobility was hampered. Whilst Western Europe was rebuilding and looking for workers, Yugoslavs were still locked at home. Approvals for foreign trips were rare, passports were seldom issued, if at all for one-time use only, and confiscated upon return.

Much later, when the unemployment situation was looking like it might undermine the political system, the government started allowing so-called guest workers to go west, primarily to Germany. Now the government hit the jackpot. At the time of greatest need, it started getting foreign currency remittances. Eventually, those remittances came to represent one third of the total foreign currency income for the State. The other third was actual exports, mostly raw materials with limited value added, and the final third was income from tourism.

> With the opening of borders, under economic pressure Yugoslavia started to drift even further away from the Soviet idea. Initially, the first break came with resolutions of Informbiro (Cominform – Communist Information Bureau, a Soviet tool to control the enslaved Eastern-European countries).
>
> In 1948 Yugoslavia was kicked out for departing from Marxism-Leninism. (Translated: not listening to Stalin's commands). But Stalin and his successors' commands – the so-called Brezhnev doctrine -- included sending Warsaw Pact tanks into the streets of Budapest and Prague. Both sides started their own purges of Titoists in eastern Europe. This included everybody who thought that their countries like Poland, Hungary, Bulgaria, Romania, East Germany, Czechoslovakia, should have similar freedom of choice like Yugoslavia. And of Informbiroist in Yugoslavia that included everybody who believed that Stalin was infallible, and knew the only correct way to pure communism. But the end-result for the Yugoslavs living there, was more freedom than what East Germany or Poland were able or prepared to offer to their citizens until the end of the 1980's.

The conflict with the Soviet Union deepened in 1961, when Tito with Nasser (Egypt), Nehru (India), Nkrumah (Ghana) and Sukarno (Indonesia) established a Non-Aligned Movement. The aim was to build a block to offer a strong voice in a world dominated by the two superpowers. Tito, cynically used this new position of power to negotiate more loans and grain deliveries from the US.

Interestingly, now that the borders were open (from the early 1960's), and nobody was being shot any more when trying to cross them, Tito's fear of flood (or, in Ross Perot's parlance: Woosh – the giant sucking sound, except, he was referring to jobs, not people), didn't materialize. However the quiet brain drain started when Western Europe recognized most of the Croatian medical and engineering university degrees. In time, the combination of "guest workers" and qualified professionals reached a third of the total working population.

Those of my less-mobile but still ambitious colleagues, opted for joining the Communist party, thereby opening venues to both promotions, and most importantly, state apartments.

Bribery on the generational scale. This mass joining of the Party was a very Yugoslav model. The Soviet Union, and later China never looked for masses to join the Party, it was always the selected and special few. In Yugoslavia, the percentage of members was around 5.8% of the population. In the USSR and PRC however, the percentages were around 1% and 0.3% respectively. Because of this watering down of the membership, the hoped-for benefits were not available to everyone.

The members became bored with discussing the glorious victories of Communism and the numerous and always changing five-year non-implementable economic plans, so they stopped showing up at party cell meetings. The only difference between members and non-members were the party dues withdrawn from members monthly checks. So, members started leaving, and the party died with a whisper, along with the death of Yugoslavia, in 1991.

From those pre-sixties times I began my obsession with passports. A passport for me (and millions of others) was not just a book, it was a pass to the free world. But it came with background checks, exit and return interviews, and could be taken away at any time, at the whim of any official. My Western friends had a problem understanding this. If and when they had a need for a passport, they would mail in a request and get it back in a few weeks' time.

So, to calm my nerves, later I got myself several additional ones: Austrian, based on my family's roots in the Austrian-Hungarian Empire, and American, after working and living here for eleven years. By now, both my Croatian and Austrian passports had expired, together with my phobias.

My wife Jadranka, was born in Zagreb, and as a baby was brought to Dubrovnik, on the Adriatic coast. Her family was still there, but slowly all passed away. First her father, who never recovered from his prison time, then her brother, and eventually, her mother.

Jadranka returned to Zagreb for her University degree (in languages), got a job at IBM and stayed. This is where I first met her. She was the librarian there. Apparently, I had very little interest in the IBM library (or so she said), so I seldom visited, and beyond exchanging a few words, we never had any serious contact. Sometime later, she left for a better job, and I hadn't seen her again until I joined Sperry Univac. She was working for the Univac representative company in Zagreb. There is where we eventually got together. We married in 1977.

Jadranka came into the marriage with a jewel, a summer home on the coast (Lozica) overlooking a few islands, including the infamous Daksa, which I've previously mentioned, and the Adriatic Sea. The view was spectacular as far as the eye could see, almost to Italy. That became our retreat for all the years we spent overseas. Each year we would return and recharge, invite our friends to spend time with us, and spend time catching up on the events of the previous twelve months.

The home was not situated on a big plot, but it had figs, oranges, rosemary, lavender and grapes in late summer. And in nearby restaurants were all the fresh fish, scampi, and lobsters. Not surprisingly, despite the gigantic problems with maintaining the property from four thousand miles away, we never wanted to sell it, until in 2015, I did. After all, it was Jadranka's hometown. I had no roots there, and nobody who would take care of the place.

View from our terrace in Dubrovnik: The infamous Daksa Island

---

1. *See book by Nikolai Tolstoi: Minister and the Massacres. MacMillan was the allied political figure in charge of the liberated territory of Austria and Italy.*

11

BIG TOE, SLOWLY, IN CAPITALISM

Up until I moved to the Far East, specifically Hong Kong, I wasn't fully immersed in the capitalist system. I worked for an American corporation in various staff jobs in the UK and Holland, and ran the Yugoslav operation, but most of that was still in the shadow of Yugoslavia – a hybrid experience.

As the Managing Director of Sperry Asia, with three divisions (Vickers, Sperry Marine and Sperry Univac), and the manager of Sperry Univac South East Asia operations, I wasn't only responsible for the computer operations, but also had fiduciary duties towards the local HM Crown Colony Government. Payroll, taxes, labor laws, export and import licenses, pension funds and medical coverage were all a set-up differently from what I experienced in the Yugoslav system.

I thought I had kissed communism good-bye, and actually did for a while working in Indonesia, India, Thailand, Taiwan, Malaysia, and Singapore, until China came on the horizon.

On my first business trip to Canton and Peking[1] in late 1978, I thought I'd been there, done that. Only this was much, much bigger. Export-Import companies trying to avoid contact with end users, handlers and minders were everywhere, and it took endless time to negotiate contracts and to process foreign currency approvals.

Chairman Deng Xiaoping officially introduced his reforms on the 18th of December 1978. But China didn't change overnight. It wasn't a light switch, which you just push up or down. The only change I saw the following January, was that one could get an ice-tray with a drink, but not yet an ice bucket. There were also more people fluent in German, mostly engineers, who appeared in meetings with the export-import companies. All cadres trained in East Germany and during the Mao Tse Tung's Cultural Revolution, were sent to the countryside for ten or more years of reeducation. Their electrical engineering experience stopped at vacuum valves. Transistors and semiconductors were not a subject taught in the rice fields. From that time comes a small anecdote worth sharing:

> Since all the Chinese we came into contact with in the late seventies wore only their military-like tunic with

no insignia, we started guessing their ranks, to understand who was who. There were several formulas offered for example, two breast pockets and two side pockets, beats just two side pockets. But that turned out unreliable. Eventually, we had a winter solution to the puzzle (it didn't work in summer). Those shaking cold hands on arrival to the meetings, came on bicycles, those with warm hands, were driven in a limo. Fairly soon, those with warmer hands started arriving in western suits.

At that time, Peking was full of "old China hands", mainly British, Japanese and a few Europeans. Americans were waiting at the doors until Nixon's warm-up of the relationship with the PRC. I was the only American Corp. representative able to enter, on the basis of my Yugoslav passport. The Chinese were more than happy to see me: Nansilafu – a Yugoslav, subject of the only country in Europe with whom they had a warm, brotherly relationship[2]. They were interested in the workers' self-management experiment, and in me they got a court-certified (sic!) source of information.

But that love affair didn't last long. Once the US got omnipresent, Yugoslavia dropped off the horizon. We really didn't have anything to offer except a foothold in the West, and now with the US here, we were no longer needed. In the meantime, every American manager and salesman saw billions of Chinese, each buying a computer, a car, and a TV set. One of each.

That didn't materialize instantly, in the meantime, the American market got flooded with plastic dolls and Venetian gondolas with red lanterns. On the higher tech side, the key phrase was "transfer of technology". Starting 51 years ago, and until recently nobody did a thing about it. It was smooth sailing for the Chinese. On one hand, American executives were prepared to sell their first-born for a chunk of that billion person market, especially if it was close to the end of the fiscal quarter. On the other hand, the Chinese had willing helpers in their overseas folks. As opposed to the other communist countries, notably the Soviet Union and Yugoslavia, who looked at every one of their citizens who left the paradise as a spy, traitor and potential state enemy. The Chinese welcomed their expats. Their sons came back to help the country in need. They returned with investment, expertise and technology transfers, sometimes not exactly totally legal, as it was shown recently.

> In those early days, nobody was making much money in China, except the Chinese. Available office space didn't exist, and that was the area where the Chinese first applied the marked economy rules of demand and supply. If the demand was one hundred, and supply was zero, then there was nothing wrong with the price being a million. After the initial installation

of mainframe computers, we needed support staff permanently stationed in China. There were only two hotels in Peking open to foreigners. The Peking hotel (Beijing Fan Dian) and the Friendship hotel.

The Friendship was a dump, infested with cockroaches. I still had to book my best friend Fred Davies, there. He discovered that sleeping with the lights on would keep the pests away. If we managed to get a room in the Peking hotel for some of our dignitaries we wouldn't vacate the room, once our guests left. Instead we turned it into an office, at an exorbitant daily room rate. Of course, today the situation has changed completely. Office blocks and new hotels were built. The Peking hotel was renovated into Deluxe class, and the Friendship hotel has four and a half stars. Gone are the days when a cube of ice for a drink was a charge of an additional dollar.

Other sources of income were taxis, actually "limos". There were only two models, one that looked like a Russian Moskwich (it probably was a knock-off), for normal dignitaries, and one larger, similar to Russian ZIL limousines, for real dignitaries. You didn't hire a cab just for a ride. There was no need for taxis because everybody had a bicycle, or so it seemed. Cars were hired for the day, or the month. All were state owned. There was no private competition, because there were no private cars, which in itself was a good reason, and in a capital city of 6 million people, there were no public gas stations.

Due to no competition or free market price formation, charges were high. The story of the lack of gas stations was driven home very illustratively. Our corporate president visited China and was taken to the Great Wall. On the way he started feeling unwell, not a surprising result of eating food he wasn't exposed to before, nor could he remember the name of it, or even pronounce it. So, he asked that the driver be told that when he taps him on the shoulder, he should take the car to the nearest gas station (euphemism for toilet). Well, the interpreter said, there are no gas stations in China. But lots of corn fields. I used the story later, when arguing for a hardship posting supplement for our employees.

Like everybody else, we got into the game of selling some computer systems, and giving some away. The business was churning along, but we never saw the computer-in-every-household success. On that front, I eventually realized that you must either give away all your family jewels, or settle for a very, very long-term (expensive) presence.

China was not my only challenge. The other one was India. Although it had some 600 million inhabitants, somehow nobody was talking about a computer in every household. Maybe because of the lack of power, sewage systems, and freshwater.

The largest democracy in the world had some serious tasks to address, and yes, computerization was but one. Not yet on the personal computer level. Actually, word processors of any kind were forbidden, and large pools of typists, almost all men, were typing away on their typewriters, with twelve sheets of papers and carbon sheets in between. Contract negotiations and agreements took days to write, even weeks, because every change in the text required a total rewrite. But it kept employment high – hence the PC proscription.

We had some commercial success in India, notably the computerization of Air India operations, but nothing comparable to the size of the country and actual cost of operating there.

I went to Agra, saw the Taj Mahal, and to Bangalore, to see the Indian Silicon Valley. Little did I know in the 1970's, that twenty years later we would be buying the brainpower there, for our software developments. Bombay and Hyderabad were next, hoping to get a foothold into the defense and aircraft industries. But India was, like Brazil one of the up-and-coming giants where governments believed their own propaganda. They spread it around the world, and many journalists fell for it. The New York Times' Thomas Friedman was one who was predicting India's economy overtaking the

US economy some 10 years ago – The Earth is Flat, (2005).

These countries continue to keep their position of up-and-coming, and not much will change until they embrace a real market economy and free investments, without government meddling. With their markets closed to direct foreign investments, they closed themselves to state-of-the art technologies, and were draining the last drops of profits. In case of Brazil, they were still making the first generation personal computers, not allowing new generation computers to enter the country, That caused them to actually lose step with technological developments.

The same happened with the endless run of the VW Beetle manufacturing line. India did similarly, with their car industry. Morris and Austin cars, models around 1956-1957, were omnipresent and were cars of choice for taxies.

Almost always one would be picked up from the airports of New Delhi or Bombay by one of these taxis with a driver and a co-pilot. When queried about it, the drivers called them "my brother". It turned out that the brothers were very useful in pushing the car, when the little 37 horsepower engine gave up. On one occasion, I went to pick up my boss Fred Davies, at the airport. I insisted on leaving the brother behind as there were, in that small car already two of us, plus driver and the luggage. The revenge was instant. Fred and I ended up pushing the car.

Then the world changed. Today, Jaguar is an Indian company. They have an enormous homegrown car industry. Brazil's government made a 180 degree turn on foreign technology investments, plus they discovered oil which aided their economy greatly. Both countries are members of BRIC, another up-and-coming giant, consisting of Brazil, Russia, India and China. They later added South Africa. When the name was coined, promises were high. Today, only two economies are firing on all cylinders, China and India.

In other Far Eastern countries we worked through dealers and distributors. India, Singapore and Hong Kong were exceptions, with Singapore and Hong Kong being fully owned subsidiaries of Sperry. In India, per law we had an agent. Mostly, the operations were owned by influential individuals in their respective societies, and not surprisingly, most of our business came from the governments. On one hand, that's where the money was, but on the other hand, they were tough clients. Almost as a rule, police, army and airline operations were run by active or retired generals. They were a group of people not generally known as open to compromises, or for bending their opinions.

> On the subject of our local partners, the most interesting personality and by far the richest, was C.Y.

Tung (Tung Chao Yung). His son in law Roger King, was married to Tung's daughter Alice. He ran the Taiwan distributorship. C.Y. and was originally from China. He came with Chang Kai Shek to Taiwan in 1949 and arrived eventually, via Hong Kong and London to the USA, on the Queen Elisabeth I.

On that trip he decided that next time he had to cross the Atlantic, he would do it on the Queen Elisabeth I as the owner, not a paying passenger.

So, he bought the ship.

He later turned her into a floating university called Seawise University, which was a play on his initials. He became a major shipping magnate. Dubbed the "Onassis of the Orient", with a large fleet of crude carriers (Orient Overseas Line), and building the world's largest oil tanker (by cutting a large one in half and adding a segment) and having it flown under the Taiwanese flag to promote his adopted country.

The Queen Elisabeth I turned out to be too big and too expensive for her purpose, and one day in the Hong Kong harbor, she caught fire simultaneously in five places, and sank. She is still there and the aficionados of James Bond movies may remember the Man with the Golden Gun scene where Roger Moore visits the MI5 office located underwater in the ship's hold.

C.Y. invited us to a screening of the movie which he had shot about the fire on the Queen Elisabeth I. By sheer coincidence, the helicopters and the filming crews were ready at hand, when the fire started.

Earlier I mentioned how The Peoples' Republic welcomed back all their overseas Chinese. C.Y.'s was an extreme example. He opted for the Republic of China (Taiwan), and was their honorary consul, but The People's Republic made his son, C.H. Tung (Tung Chee Hwa), the first Governor and Chief Executive of the new Special Administrative Region, Hong Kong.

Another example, along similar lines would be the Kadoorie family. Although not Chinese, their adopted home from the 1880's, was Shanghai. Once the richest people there, they left before the Communist takeover in 1949. They stayed in Hong Kong, amassed a new fortune (the old one was confiscated) and waited. Once China started opening, they were the first ones to be called back to help, beginning with building the first nuclear power plant. From then on, they went on to building the Peninsula hotel in Shanghai, and so on. The pragmatic Chinese didn't mind that they were first-class capitalists. They were the old China hands, never went against the PRC, and were welcomed back, for their knowledge and abilities, not their political views.

Again, I spent most of my time traveling. The area was vast, from Jakarta and Manila, to Delhi, Bombay, Taipei and Peking (see the map at the back). But this time my marriage survived well and I had great support from my wife Jadranka. She not only looked after me, but also after the bunch of displaced expats and their wives, who came to work in Hong Kong. The Company was paying for their children's education back home, typically in the UK, but that was a double-edged sword. They did get a good education, but families were split and lots of frustration was apparent.

In Hong Kong we built a big circle of friends, and when not sailing, would socialize with them. One group were Cyprus "refugees", pilots from Cyprus Airways who left the island in 1974, once Turkey invaded it. Mostly British and some Australians, now flying for Cathay Pacific.

Our home, in Chung Hom Kok became again, like our former apartment in Zagreb, a place where friends would congregate. Besides the flying crowd like Patrick and Jeanne Preston, there were people whom we originally met through business, like Peter and Jill James.

An anecdote about Peter, a well-educated product of the British public school system, did eight years of studying Latin. On a business trip to Rome, he jumped into taxi at the airport and tried to get to his hotel. Not speaking

Italian, he tried his Latin words. The taxi driver said Bene, bene, and took him directly to the Vatican.

OTHER FRIENDS we originally met through business were Arthur Young, or Paul and Beverlee Travers, from Cable and Wireless, and some sailing friends, like Ike and Cindy Ambrose. One of the people who spent a lot of time at our place was Zdravko Mršić, my original marketing manager at IBM, who joined me at Univac in 1972. I offered him a marketing manager job in the South East organization, and he accepted. Roles reversed a bit, but that turned out not to be a problem.

A dinner in Chung Hom Kok: from r.: Zdravko, Jim and Zdeni Ellis, Fred, Malina self and Jadranka

Of course, I was accused of bringing in my mafia. I brought in my former Croatia branch manager from the original Yugoslav operation, John Lilywhite. I found in place my former Slovenia branch manager Jim Ellis, who was at that time running the Singapore branch. So, there was a clique of my former colleagues in the operation and honestly, I saw nothing wrong with having somebody to watch "my six".

Once I left Hong Kong, they dispersed as well. John went on to run a solar panel manufacturing business in the US, Jim joined the Sperry operation in Perth, Australia and Zdravko went into a private consulting business in Holland. Today, Jim is still in Perth. Zdravko switched to politics and became the first Croatian minister of foreign affairs, and started his own political party. He eventually retired, and is now writing books on mostly political economy and anti-globalization.

Whilst in Hong Kong, I was also involved with various local managers on issues of importance to our respective companies, like payroll laws and regulations, pension fund management and issues of training and recruitment of professional staff. That generated an invitation to join educational and professional institutions, like the Institute of Management. Eventually, I got my "letters" – a very British system of memberships and fellowships, a bit popular in the United States and not at all in Europe. That's how I ended up with FBIM and FInstAM designations.

. . .

After a bit more than four years, my managers back in the States decided that it was time for me to move again. The big difference between the British and American approach to foreign assignments is, the British management believes in longevity of the postings. So many managers of for example, Cable and Wireless and Standard Charter Bank, two large British organizations, have been in Hong Kong for almost twenty years. While the American managers believe in shuffling their people around. Large British companies eventually split their management teams and once one becomes a part of the overseas department, a return to domestic is almost impossible.

Not so with the US companies. In my own example, I twice accepted a job back "home" after foreign assignments. Four years for a rotation appeared to be an unwritten standard. It was not a great formula for building long lasting customer business relationships, or developing friendships, but by now being a professional expat, I was slowly getting used to this. The American approach had one great side-benefit. We always had a lot of welcoming and farewell parties. I myself had two of each in Hong Kong.

---

1. *Throughout the text I used Chinese names of people and places in usage at the time when I visited them. Hence Peking, Canton, Mao Tse-Tung. Later, China told the world how to spell, and the world kowtow.*
2. *PRC's relationship with other European Communist countries and the USSR, was cool. They liked Yugoslavia's, more individual approach to Communism, than the* diktat *from Moscow.*

12

AMERICA, HERE WE COME

So, in 1982 it was off to headquarters in Blue Bell, Pennsylvania. With so much time spent overseas, reeducation was in order to avoid the managers going native. I was put in charge of the marketing department covering most of the world except Europe and North America. So, it was Africa, Asia, Australia, and South America.

In this new job, I became fairly familiar with most of the international and local Univac operations. We settled in a nice area, Valley Forge. We purchased a house, with ¾ of an acre of lawn to be mowed, leaves to be raked, snow shoveled, a dog, and a green card. It looked like we were settled forever. I even got myself a big Cadillac Eldorado, like the ones I had seen as a kid, in the movies. It was bigger than the sailing sloop I had in Yugoslavia, where we would sail, cook, eat and sleep for two weeks at a time.

A pride of house ownership: first load of some twenty bags of raked leaves.

THE JOB, like all my previous and future jobs, included a lot of travelling and crisscrossing the globe. I raked up a million miles on Pan Am, United, and many on the local airlines, primarily Cathay Pacific. I lived in a permanent state of jet-lag.

The dog hated me because I would walk it at unholy hours. I was awake at night and tired during the day. All discussions with the management of our Australian and Asian operations were taking place during nighttime hours, the time-difference being some 12 hours. I still had to look after my old patch Asia, and had to become familiar with and begin working with our operations in Australia and South America.

Our operations in Africa shrank with the changes in Rhodesia, to a single subsidiary, being South Africa. But at least Johannesburg was not twelve time-zones away. The good news with our neighbors down south, was that we were in the same or similar zones.

Thinking back, I see that I spent most of my time working with the marketing teams of Mexico and Australia. Both were well functioning operations, with local management well established in business circles. Interestingly, in South Africa we never managed to establish local management. For years, most of our managers were expatriates. Morney Mahoney was at least a South African born American.

It was similar in Brazil, but business there was more promises than actual success. Their insistance on local content, barter, and transfer of technology was the biggest problem. But at least the South African operations had an impressive installed base, that was almost entirely government and banks, where the money was.

A reward I received out of these trips to faraway places, that enabled me to get a good impression of the region, was the chance to do some sailing. With Royal Cape club, and Rio's Iate Clube de Rio, my club RHKYC had reciprocal privileges. In Melbourne, our company had an employees' owned large sailing boat ready to go.

Back home, I started revisiting my career options and thought about throwing my hat into the ring, when the company was looking for a new head of International operations. From my time in London and Amsterdam, I was already pretty familiar with most of the European operations, and I would be bringing to the job the newly acquired experience from the rest of the world (minus Canada. I got involved there later). But the powers that be had different designs for me. Trouble was brewing with our business in the Far East, both in China and Hong Kong, and in 1984 I was sent back to Asia.

As I said in the beginning of this chapter, we thought we were settling in the States forever. But in Sperry parlance "forever" is an elastic term, and lasted for us, only two years.

13

SECOND TIME IN HONG KONG

Originally, I was told to move to Singapore. This time, I was to run the operation out of there. Somebody in the US HQ decided that this was the place to be. It apparently looked good on the map, or a glossy magazine. There was no way I would do that. For four years I was the visiting managing director of the local operation there. I had problems with the sterility of the place, the nominal democracy, or nominal dictatorship, whichever you want to choose, obsessive cleanliness, and rules for every step one wants to make.

I read somewhere that every employee had a right to say NO, the only thing being, nobody knew, how many times. Management even worked on my wife, but she stood by me. Eventually, the marching orders were changed to Hong Kong.

Apparently, we had more problems with low revenue, high cost and low profitability, than with the location of my office. Additionally, I was promised to be brought back to the US, and offered something exciting, an actual term; not more than two years or "until you fix it".

Of course, me returning to Hong Kong raised some eyebrows. One is not supposed to return to the scene of the crime. Local newspapers, in the economic section, carried an article about management change in the local Sperry organization, saying tongue in cheek, that Sperry brought in R. Fischer, as a manager -- again. But our friends, whom we left behind were happy. And most importantly, our customers didn't forget me.

The first boost to business came with the successful installation of a large computer system, and implementation of various airline applications at Cathay Pacific, the local premium airline. I even got a new license plates for the company car, showing CX 1700, CX being the airline code and 1700 the car's mobile phone number. Few other deals followed. Most importantly, we renewed our friendship with Ike and Cindy Ambrose and got into a partnership with them, sailing their Formosa ketch. But that is part of a different story, for later. In China, we refocused on building local operations, with local personnel, to lower the cost of support.

As mentioned earlier, technology transfer was high on the Peoples' Republic agenda. We saw an opportunity to do a bit of knowledge transfer in exchange for some preferential treatment in the educational field procurements. We offered to donate one of our mainframes, software and maintenance training to an educational entity, in order for them to start a data processing service business, and help us eventually with training and maintenance of the systems we sold.

We thought at least that the donation part wouldn't be a problem. We even brought in some heavy hitters, like the head of International operations, Joe Ciasullo, to add decorum, cut ribbon, and drink mai tais. But it took him, and his aides, a full week to give away the computer system. In the process he learned patience (not easy for an Italian), and to eat sea cucumbers, and similar creatures. Eventually, he got rid of that computer, but never forgave me for inviting him to Peking.

Later, following a Joint Venture agreement with CITIC[1] (signed and celebrated in the newly opened *Maxim's*, of all places), we met with the Vice Premier of the PRC, Mr. Peng, who eventually became Premier in 1987. We got the full treatment, a large limo decorated with the Sperry company flag – not that Moskwich knock-off from Chapter 11, tea sipping and a photo-op in the Great Hall of the People.

Pick-up for the meeting in the Great Hall of People

With the Vice Premier in the Great Hall of People

THE MOST IMPORTANT development was a breakthrough into the Chinese airline industry. In 1985 we signed a contract for computerizing most of the various activities of the Chinese airline CAAC. That included a multiprocessing computer system, passenger service, cargo operation, revenue enhancement applications, etc. Things went well and my organization and I were, after a year, selected as the Subsidiary and the General Manager of the year (with a handshake and a wink: sit tight).

True to their word, the company came through and decided to send me to Japan to look after Sperry interests in our joint venture there. As a bonus, I got enrolled for the summer in the European management school, INSEAD in Fontainebleau, France. I gorged on Indian business cases, French wine and food, and weekends in the country. That was the time when Indian postgrads started flooding business schools worldwide, as well as the American business schools and the mathematical departments of all major American universities. But for me it was time to leave the charming French environment and face the challenge of a new cultural environment, Japan.

---

1. *CITIC, China International Trade and Investment Corp., is one more case showing the pragmatism of the PRC leaders: The Chairman of CITIC, Ron Yi Reng was never a Party member, but one of the gang of Shanghai capitalists, who survived the 1949 regime change. He got enormous power over foreign investments, and PRC had minimal interest in his political orientation.*

14

THE LAND OF RISING SUN

After a great summer in France, I was ready to confront my joint venture partners, Mitsubishi, OKI Electric, and the almighty Mitsui Corp. Boy, did my time in China prepare me!

I knew handshaking was not appropriate, neither was the Russian and French style three kisses, and small talk was also not in *vogue*. Like the Chinese, my Japanese hosts were able to sit for hours just staring and expecting a foreigner to eventually talk, and say something he never planned to say.

Even without foreigners, that game of chicken is played over and over in Japan. Body language reveals more than words. Apparently, I passed the shut-up-and-be-quiet test. The JV partners accepted Sperry Univac's recommendation and voted to have me appointed to the Board of NUK Nippon Univac Kaisha, and offered to appoint me as Fukushacho, or Executive Vice President, which is the equivalent of the American COO, Chief Operating Officer.

So, I entered the world of consensus. Preparations for the Board meetings took at least two to three times the time allocated to the actual meetings. Issues were, in a most monotone way, presented by lower level managers. Few, if any members asked questions, and the proposal was put to vote, with the expected 100% approval. Since all the heavy lifting was done before by the staff of various interested parties, the Board members had only one task, to say, "Hay". Then they all withdrew to a sushi and sake lunch.

As a Board member, I assumed responsibility for the one thousand person R&D department. It was the same approach here. I wasn't bothered with making big decisions, issues were long settled by the time they came to the top floor. However, my job description, as the Sperry Univac Vice president in charge of our one-third interests in the venture (my other hat), was to protect Univac's position in the market. Here, the R&D department played an important role. The combination of these two roles of mine was a perfect prescription for constant friction.

The Sperry position, the one I was trying to implement, was if the JV needed some equipment, Sperry would build or procure it, at the best prices and or conditions.

The JV position was that they would get it, from as a rule, a Japanese source. Be it hardware, software, supplies, it didn't matter.

Involvement with R&D got me involved directly connected with the issue of quality control. There are many reasons why Japanese products conquered the world, but probably number one would be (after the initial assault on the American market in the fifties and sixties, with cheap and shoddy products), the quality of the wares they offered.

Books were written about the comparison of American and Japanese car qualities, but that discrepancy was visible in every product. Similar to the push for exports, quality was another religion, or maybe just an offshoot of the same religion, that the Japanese practiced. I was invited, and gladly accepted participation in a Total Quality Control International workshop.

The workshop was led by prof. Kaoru Ishikawa, the father of the TQC. He built his "T" (from Total) on the scientific foundation of the E. Deming's QC, adding Japanese specifics of devotion, group responsibility, and quality circles. The knowledge I took with me, I later applied in my own development center in Minneapolis, when going for a quality certification (see Chapter 15)

The JV was expected to promote the interest of all partners in the Joint Venture. So, our offices, including the future HQ, were located in buildings leased from, and owned by Mitsui Real Estate Corp. Most of our electronic components were procured locally, and of course, what was available, from OKI Electric, another JV partner.

But when it came to computer peripherals, the company was looking far and wide for non-US, Japanese replacements. Computer discs (preferably Hitachi), were the number one turf battle, then came UNIX workstations. I have to admit that at that time, SUN stations were a superior product to anything we had to offer, and the Hitachi discs' MTBF (meantime between failures) of some 240,000 hours was something nobody could match.

Not IBM, not us. But in life, one plays the cards that one is dealt, not the ones one would wish one had. After all, NUK was not an independent company, but a designated distributor for Sperry Univac data processing systems.

The late 1980's was a time of newly born Japanese nationalism. Not of the 1930's militaristic kind, but mostly focused on the economy.

Japanese exports were exploding. They couldn't make enough automobiles to satisfy the American appetite. Japanese electronics flooded the US, their trade imbalance with the US was climbing through the roof. Their stock market as well.

NIKKEI stock index closed in 1989 at a peak of 38,915. That was the time when "Buy Japanese" wasn't a slogan, but a marching order. That was the time when Shintaro Ishihra's[1] book: "The Japan That Can Say NO" came out. That was the time when the joint striker F-16 fiasco started (it later nicely recovered), and Toshiba gave the American quiet submarine propeller technology to the Soviets. Also, it was the time when the helpless American congressmen were smashing Toshiba radios on the Capitol Hill.

One of the problems was Japanese exclusions of US supercomputers from Japanese institutes and universities, whilst at the same time they started penetrating the US scientific market. Ronald Regan's Commerce department started some activities to level the playing field, and in 1988 put together the first delegation to start negotiations with Japan.

As a local "expert" I ended up in these negotiations with MITI, the Ministry of International Trade and Industry, the creators of the Japanese Industrial policy. The way the meetings were orchestrated, it was clear that we would not get anywhere. First, we all had to see and pay our respects to Mike Mansfield. He was by then US ambassador to Japan for eleven years, and the last thing he wanted to see was someone rocking the boat.

So, we got a lecture on peaceful compromises, mutual understanding, respect, thousands of years of Japanese history, cherry blossoms, and the State of Montana, where he could not wait to go back to, and retire once he left Tokyo. Of course, as with all politicians, he never went back to Montana, he settled in Washington, DC.

We then had a series of introductions to the Japanese powers that be, and were eventually sent back, without any visible result. George Bush's new Secretary Mosbacher, showed interest in taking up the general issue of trade with Japan and Korea, so he revived the supercomputer initiative.

It was another delegation, and another lack of results. But the matter resolved itself. Most of the high speed, high volume computing started being shifted to distributed processing. The mammoth computer got replaced by many thousands of processors, attacking the problems in parallel hence, Parallel Computing.

My take from that endeavor was that no negotiations will ever fix the problems in Japan, or with Korea, and not with China. The present approach by president Trump is novel. Japan and Korea, now the smaller fish, are agreeing to more balanced one-on-one trade agreements. NAFTA was replaced and China relations started to be slowly fixed, through tariffs this time. The Corona virus threw a cog into the process. We will have to see if there is going to be a continuation, or if things will go back to the beginning.

Against that background I was supposed to ensure that "our" 10,000 Japanese employees stick to promoting US imports, contrary to whatever was going on around them. This was a bit of a frustrating task, which for years to come, left on me a much stronger impression and memories of those years in Japan, than seeing the beauties of Japanese gardens, the historic capital Kyoto, or the famous Mount Fuji.

> Of course, I had to visit Hiroshima. As a student I saw the French New Wave's Hiroshima, mon amour, which left me with a romantic vision of that devastation. In the course of time I also read a lot about the Pacific war, and the deployment of that device over Hiroshima and Nagasaki. But none of that prepared me for the vastness of the destruction.
>
> The sight and the museum could have had a great educational value, showing what should be avoided, and what could happen again, if conflicts between nations are not peacefully resolved.
>
> In 1987 we were still in the midst of the Cold war, although the end to that was coming fast. However, neither the Japanese, or my hosts or a combination of the above, caused me to come out of Hiroshima telling myself that nobody, and for sure not the Japanese, learned anything from that experience.

Nowhere in the exhibits is any mention of the cause of this man-made disaster, or of the road leading to that faithful August in 1945, or of any guilt shared by the Japanese. OK, maybe of the guilt of the Japanese government, since people are always hiding behind that. The masses are innocent. Tell this to the Bataan marchers, or the victims of the rape of Nanjing. It wasn't the Emperor's ministers doing it themselves. They had their willing executioners. The whole purpose, or at least that was my feeling, was to impress on the visitors, especially Americans, the guilt about what they did to the people of Japan. I refused to feel guilty, besides everything else, I wasn't even an American subject, and I did not drop that device.

Despite all this said before, not all was fine in the kingdom of Denmark. Koreans were slowly biting at their heels, producing and outselling the Japanese in electronics. Banks were overexposed with real-estate deals, which eventually imploded, and the stock market slid to 8,148, never to recover back to the glory days of 1989. Today, 27 years after its low, it is hovering just under 20,000, about half of what it used to be.

Back home, Sperry Corporation was going through its own turbulence and was acquired by Burroughs in 1986. We in Japan were not part of that activity, having been a Joint venture with a majority (66%) Japanese ownership. But eventually, that had to be settled. After getting high priced advice from American consulting companies who knew nothing about joint ventures, or the Japanese market, for that matter, we rolled Burroughs' Japanese wholly owned subsidiary into NUK, and renamed the company to NUL, (Nihon Unisys Ltd.)

We continued our various fights, the Japanese fighting to increase the local content of the hardware they were selling and installing, and the newly named Unisys Corp., fighting to at least maintain the status quo.

Reception to introduce the newly named company Nihon Unisys Ltd., to the press and customers. From right: T. Sawachi, Chairman, K. Nishikawa, President, R.M. Fischer, Exec VP, K. Tomita, Managing Director and Y. Sugimura, Managing Director

THE NEGOTIATIONS themselves were very educational. Teams of Burroughs, Unisys Corp, Mitsui, OKI and other interested parties were put together, and NUK Board members sat on the other side waiting for the final outcome of the form of merger and incorporation.

Initially, there were three lawyers from the US Corporation and a few provided by the consultants, but NUK had none. Actually, we didn't even have ANY on our payroll, just a few paralegals. So, we got two on loan from Mitsui. If the news would have spread that a multibillion-dollar multinational merger could be done without lawyers, this would have had devastating effects on the US. But the potential pandemic didn't happen, and the Japanese continued to run their lives without the lawyers, and Americans continued to have their lives run by the lawyers.

> Life in Japan was interesting and satisfying on some levels, but frustrating on others. I already mentioned the push for the decrease of American exports was constantly present. Millions of people in a city without parks, only concrete playgrounds painted green, was the best Tokyo could offer.
>
> Japan was without vistas, parking and with horrendous traffic jams. It was exhausting. Swimming in the American Club pool was one-way, until the whistle blew then turned, and exit right!

THE LAND OF RISING SUN

Even leaving Tokyo for a weekend in Hakone which was 35 miles away, may mean a six to seven hours drive back on Sundays, on that infamous Shuto highway. After some negotiations, I was allowed to drive the company car (senior managers are driven around, they do not do the dirty work themselves). However, I was warned of a legal truth, the same that I was also told when attempting to drive in China. If you get involved in an accident, irrespective of what you may think, it's your fault.

This legal logic was explained by saying, if I wouldn't have been in China or Japan, that accident wouldn't have happened. The point was driven home when a lady hit me while my car was stationary in a parking lot, and the insurance assigned the guilt as 50/50. It was a relief that 100% fault was not assigned to me.

Another pastime was golf. Before Japan, I tried to play only a couple of times, in Europe and Hong Kong. But in Japan, I was told that this is business, not an option. A senior company manager has to spend Sundays on the course, as a host to potential or existing customers, and to visiting overseas dignitaries, whom my Japanese colleagues didn't feel like entertaining.

The company had several golf club memberships, probably worth millions of dollars, but the round of golf was still some $1,000[2]. Eighteen holes was a full day's job, starting at the crack of dawn. First a two hour ride out of town, after nine holes, a great lunch, usually sushi and sashimi, and of course, sake. The 19th hole didn't start until after a hot bath (some 104°F – 40°C), when everybody was ready for some adult drinks and dinner.

Afterwards, everybody would be driven home in their respective cars, enjoying a two hour nap. I wasn't good at golf, neither were many of my guests, but I thoroughly enjoyed walking in the open space, where the horizon wasn't less than 100 feet away, like it is in Tokyo.

We spent almost four years, (until his departure for the US) with a friend from Washington, DC. We met Juan Carlos Hrase von Bargen in 1982 in DC, through our Zagreb friend Maja, who was then with the World Bank.

Juan Carlos was Minister in the Paraguayan Embassy, and his partner Boris Blažić Metzner (another Croatian from Crikvenica) was Maja's boss, in charge of the Statistical Division of the WB. Juan Carlos was a graduate of Southwestern University and spent most of his life, from the age of 12, initially as an exchange student, in the US.

His "American" family lived in Memphis, TN, the home of Graceland. We all got together and had some great times in the Capital. We exchanged stories about the good old times. It turned out that when my father arrived in Zagreb in the late 1930's, he dated Boris' mother. She and her sister were Viennese girls, and of course he gravitated to German speaking ladies. Boris' mother even told me that I could have been her son.

I Perish the thought.

Eventually, we left for my second tour in Hong Kong. Sometime later, Juan Carlos was appointed Ambassador of the Republic of Paraguay to Japan. When we met again JC, as we called him, had two great things in Tokyo, a car with diplomatic plates, so he could park anywhere, (as opposed to normal mortals, who couldn't park anywhere), and a "crying room", where we would spend some Sunday afternoons, lamenting over life in Japan and drinking Armagnac, for medicinal purpose only, as a relaxation. JC's time in Japan was cut short when his President, Stroessner died, and he was recalled.

As A RULE, when on assignments, Jadranka and I were entertaining most of our visiting dignitaries at home. It provided a more relaxed atmosphere than in a restaurant. We could learn a lot about what was going on at Headquarters, what the latest trends were, issues the Corporation was focusing on, etc.

It also gave us, gave everybody a chance to get more familiar with each other. Some of us were running important overseas operations, and these trips were the only times when a Chairman would be able to spend more than a fleeting moment with his key employees.

We started that in Yugoslavia, with the first VP to visit E. T. Springstead, in 1976. Ted and I developed a long-lasting relationship when he took over operations covering our activities in Asia.

He offered me a job there.

We sailed several times together in the Adriatic and in Greece. Later, once he retired, in San Francisco. We even visited him in Vail, Colorado after I retired. These dinners at home continued in Hong Kong and Tokyo.

We had some exciting moments, like when Jadranka almost killed the President of the Corp., Reto Braun. He failed to mention that he was fatally allergic to cheese. And he was a Swiss! So that great Greek salad went uneaten.

The most interesting person we met at our table was Mike Blumenthal. In 1986 he became the Chairman of the newly established Unisys Corp, the result of a merger between Burroughs and Sperry. He was a frequent visitor to Japan, occasionally just passing through on his way to China (his jet couldn't make it without a stop-over), and visited with us at our home, on more than one occasion.

He had an exciting career in academia, in government, and in business. He was the US ambassador in GATT negotiations, and the Japanese remembered him well, always addressing him as Mr. Ambassador. He was Jimmy Carter's Secretary of The Treasury, who gave us 18% mortgage interest rates, as well as Chairman of Bendix and Burroughs.

I was most interested in his early days experience, since it partially paralleled my family's. He told us his story of a hurried exit from Germany in 1938, where the rounding-up of Jews was in full swing, and his father was already arrested, and sent to Dachau concentration camp.

His mother managed to get him released and with whatever funds they had left, she bought steamer tickets to Shanghai. There was no Zagreb option for them. They first had to go by train through occupied (actually annexed) Austria and then Mussolini's Italy (neither of the countries Jew-friendly), to board the ship in Naples. Shanghai was by then, the only open city to refugees, Nobody else welcomed them.

At their final destination, the Sassoons and Kadoories, the Shanghai Bund trading companies owned by Syrian Jews, established reception organizations and were helping the arriving refugees. With the large numbers, despite all the efforts, the help was inadequate, and in the end everybody had to fend for himself.

I mentioned the Kadoories earlier in Chapter 11. They, and the Sassoons were regarded by the communists as exploiters, and they wisely left Shanghai in 1949, minus all possessions. But the rest of the world who had involvement with them, looked at them in a far more positive light. Both trading houses had established charities, hospitals, and schools, to aid all the communities, local Chinese and expats.

Of course, helping the approximately 18,000 Jewish refugees was one of their most important achievements. Sassoons had a problem, their trading house was closely related to the mid-nineteen century opium wars. That mark was never erased, and after leaving Shanghai they never recovered, as opposed to the Kadoori house, as described in the earlier chapter. After the Japanese withdrew from Shanghai, Mike left for the US in 1947, richer by the experience.

He gained workable knowledge of three additional languages: Portuguese, Chinese (I don't know if Mandarin, or Wu) and English. He studied at the San Francisco college, U.C. Berkley and eventually, Princeton.

The rest is history.

During one of the dinners there was a moment of disagreement on the subject of the evils of Communism. Mike, being a liberal product of Berkley, and the Kennedy and Carter administration, held opinions, a bit left of my wife Jadranka. Next morning, he graciously mentioned that I have a wife with fairly firm opinions about East and West. With her family experience, that wasn't surprising.

---

1. *Ishihara was at that time Minister of Transportation in the government, and co-wrote the book with the chairman of Sony, Akio Morita. Later, Ishihara became mayor of Tokyo.*
2. *If this sounds a lot for a round of golf, consider the housing costs: Our three-bedroom apartment was going for $14,000 a month, and a pound of steak for $80. Grapes, sold by individual berries, 100 yen (just under a dollar) a piece. Japan was an expensive place to live in.*

15

BACK IN THE STATES

In 1989 I got a new boss, Reto Braun, who became president following a series of changes at the top of the Corporation. Blumenthal was still running the company, but was about to leave for Lazard Freres, and then Berlin to become the head of the new Jewish Museum.

> The merger was far from being successful. They had non-compatible product lines, no synergy and both companies had declining market shares. Both had heavy dependence on mainframes at the time the world was going distributed. They didn't have any personal computer offerings, and worse of all, no vision on the top. That was an ill, dating back many years.

At a press conference in Peking in 1985, then Sperry Chairman Probst, waived away a journalist's question about PCs as a fad, soon to be over. At the time of the merger, the combined company who for a short time was going under the name NuCo, had a total of 260,000 employees. After shedding most of the non-computer businesses (see Notes), and drastically pairing down the payroll, it eventually settled on some 20,000 today. Blumenthal saw the light early, but it took some time for me to realize which way my career was going.

Reto agreed to my request to be returned Stateside for a new position in the corporation. By then, I had enough of Japan. Besides other reasons, I wanted to eventually regulate my status, and after eight years of green-carding, I wanted to apply for United States citizenship.

Another reason was that I felt the days of our Joint Venture in Japan were numbered. The company, or at least the Unisys connection to it, became a victim of its success. NUL was now the second largest foreign computer company in Japan. It counted almost all the major players as its customers. All Nippon Airways, Nissan, Toyota, Tokyo Electric, a series of large banks, etc. were all NUL customers. As such, its market value (it was, and still is listed on the Tokyo Stock Exchange), was so attractive that Unisys started looking to cash out. One option was to sell at least a part of its holdings. Eventually, they did.

In 1993. I was sworn in as a US citizen, and invited to give a speech on behalf of the group, in the City Hall of Philadelphia

MY NEW JOB included world-wide responsibilities for marketing and development of the airline and telecommunication industry segment. Since the late 1960's, Univac was developing application software for the airline industry, and by the time I joined the division, many of the world airlines were our clients.

United, Lufthansa, Air India, CAAC, Cathay Pacific, Air France, Aeroflot, JAT, to name a few. We had installed the Reservation Systems, the dreaded Baggage Revenue

Systems (where overweight fees were calculated and fees assessed on the spot, at the time of check-in), the equally ugly Revenue Enhancement Systems (giving the airline the ability to continually change seat prices, based on supply and demand), the Cargo Systems (calculations of fees, loads etc.), Frequent Flier Systems, and a series of smaller applications.

The telecommunication area was a newly exploding market segment. Companies were transitioning from your grandfathers' rotary dialing phones, to new wireless networks, and looking for value added applications. We had several "old" customers, the largest being SITA (Société Internationale de Télécommunications Aéronautiques, HQ in Genève, Switzerland), providing telecommunications services to its 400 co-owners, working in 197 countries.

The nineties were not the time to enjoy the past successes. Our airline applications were all based on large Univac mainframes, and the user was moving towards distributed processing and small workstations. Our development center in Minneapolis tried to cope with that, but the legacy systems were a millstone around our neck. Mostly written in "old" languages (Assembly, FORTRAN), the systems were expensive to maintain and required excessive man hours. 90% of our work was system maintenance. My focus was on increasing stability and consequently increasing customer satisfaction. We embarked, as the first division in Unisys, on obtaining

ISO 9001 certification. I managed to do that, and got my picture taken with the Chairman, one more for the ego-wall.

The additional change in the marketplace was that many of the large airlines were looking to outsource their Data Processing operations, and joining trade groups like Sabre (based on AA software) and Gemini (mainly supported by AF) in Europe. Unisys lost out to IBM in the bid for our equipment to be used for the European system. So, my development group started a slow attrition process, heavily depending on support of the old applications. Things could have gone like that forever, and to my best knowledge, many of the systems are still alive and in use.

Returning to the States after leaving back in 1984, meant looking up old friends and renewing friendships. Although, I always made certain that during my occasional visits, I would get in touch with people whom we'd left behind. Our home in Devon became a place of many get-togethers and almost all New Years' celebrations.

Only a few months before the end of my career with Unisys, for some reason unclear to me, I was enrolled into Wharton Business School, for a management training seminar. Some wires got crossed somewhere, as the development further below shows. I met interesting people, both students and the faculty, and really enjoyed sitting in the classroom again. The most interesting part was how management courses had changed from my time in INSEAD. There was now heavy emphasis on group-think, on outsourcing, on just-in-time, and on ISO quality discipline and certification.

> At approximately that time, my application for naturalization was approved and I was granted American Citizenship. One of the biggest benefits was the right to vote. Up until then, I'd voted only once in my life, in Communist Yugoslavia. That was very exciting. Four names were on the ballot for four openings, people I never heard of, and my duty was to mark all the names. A very limited choice. After that experience, I never went back to vote, although voting was compulsory, but never enforced. Nobody cared. Participation was always reported as 99.5%.
>
> Now in The United States, I started to enthusiastically follow election campaigns and presented myself every second November at the ballot box. Voting is a right not many Americans use. Midterm elections are called successful if 15% of the electorate shows up. As opposed to a communist system, many decisions can be influenced by the voting population, but somehow, one does not appreciate much if this benefit is just handed to them. The fact that this right was forcefully fought for some 230 years ago, is already forgotten.

Left: Vera and Norman, right: my cousin Ursi from Graz, visiting in Devon

Not long after my return to Blue Bell, one sunny day in 1993, both Reto Braun and I were offered an opportunity to widen our horizons and look for gainful employment elsewhere. Of course, all was done in a very civilized way. We both voluntarily resigned, and even had farewell parties, then faded away. Reto returned to Switzerland, and I stayed in Devon, PA. Just shortly before that in March, my father died in Graz, Austria. I managed to attend his funeral.

And that was the end of my professional career.

Whilst still with Unisys and traveling between various airlines, airline conferences and commuting between Blue Bell, Pennsylvania and Minneapolis, where the development center was, trouble was brewing in my homeland.

Yugoslavia disintegrated and the former Yugoslav army and Serbian irregulars occupied parts of Croatia, trying to dismember it. Dubrovnik, an eight century UN World Heritage walled city was bombed and held under siege for almost a year.

Other parts of Croatia, including the capital city of Zagreb, were also bombed. The East Coast local chapter of alumni of the University of Zagreb in Philadelphia, started a campaign of raising awareness of the atrocities in Croatia. They used public gatherings in Philadelphia, and showed exhibitions of pictures of the destruction of cultural heritage sites, churches, museums, libraries and graves (many taken by my brother-in-law, Miro Kerner), in Washington, DC and on the West Coast.

They collected funds for the support of children whose parents vanished in that war. My wife Jadranka was managing this effort from this side, but like many other things, eventually its success was its undoing. The wife of the President of Croatia saw it as an attractive promotion tool, put her name on it, and took over the distribution of money.

Children started writing letters complaining of funds having dried out, and the effort died. The good old times of communist meddling never went away. After all, the President himself was a former Yugoslav army general, and a Communist party member for most of his adult life.

Eventually, Croatia emerged independent, internationally recognized, and began rebuilding. Many from the Diaspora were ready to help, and I received a call to come for an interview with the President, for a job helping with the Country's privatization activities (remember, all in Yugoslavia was State owned, and bankrupt).

My wife was excited about going home after all the years in the Far East and the US, but my mother-in-law, when asked, said, "Sure kids, it's a fantastic idea, I would love to have you here, but maybe it's too early to come back yet."

She was right. The eventual appointee survived less than six months. Corruption was rampant and steamrolled everything and everybody in its way. In the course of the various activities, we met a series of Croatians living in the area, and kept contacts for many years to come with Radovan Bubanj, a Zagreb physician with whom we had many common friends back home, Slavko and Viktorija Brkich. Eventually, Radovan's wife was our matchmaker and bridesmaid and Slavko the Best man, when Tessa and I got married in 2015.

SINCE THIS ROUNDS UP my professional career, I have a couple of observations. By working for Univac/Unisys over twenty years, I was posted in many places, in Europe, Asia and the States. I regard myself as a social animal, and made friends in most of the countries I lived in, and continued the contacts until the present day.

The exceptions were Hong Kong and Japan. The only Chinese contact we kept from Hong Kong would be K. (Kuan) Wong, the Hong Kong HR manager, who moved to the States. That's where we actually spent time together. In Japan, in all the years I was there, we were invited to only two Japanese homes. Once by a colleague with whom I sailed in the Sea of Japan, and the other was a business acquaintance, not from the same company.

Both of these societies were totally closed, and didn't have a desire for intruders. To be fair, friendship requires investments and commitments from both sides, but to befriend Americans meant a high investment at a questionable return, since we all got reassigned after short stints, never to be seen again. Additionally, the Japanese explanation was that their living conditions are such as not to allow for socializing. So the few other

Japanese homes we saw were from mixed marriage couples.

To get more immersed, I even began studying Japanese, and became pretty good at the language. Very few Japanese in the service industry (shopkeepers, taxi drivers, waiters) spoke or understood any foreign language, so to survive, some basic Japanese was a must. I never learned more than a few kanji signs, but managed the hiragana and katakana script, with 46 characters each. So, my reading and writing skills were on the level of an eight-year-old kid. That's how the Japanese children learn the script, starting with hiragana and slowly moving into kanji characters. And don't believe for a moment that the hiragana signs and names in the underground stations are for the foreigners, they are there for the school kids. To read newspapers, knowledge of some 2,000 characters is needed. So, I was 4.6% there, hardly even enough, for reading headlines.

> Whilst in Hong Kong, we met and kept company with only one Yugoslav couple, Tonči Radica, the head of Cargill's Ship management company and nephew of Dika Radica, the author and the Grand lady of Dalmatian cooking.
>
> The real cook in the family was Tonći's wife Gordana. They moved to Norway, where Gordana was teaching local ladies the mysteries of other foods beyond norske fiske and boiled chicken and potatoes.

However, in Tokyo it was different. We met several interesting people from Yugoslavia, and stayed in contact with some of them for a long time after leaving Japan. One couple were Ešo and Ariana Abadžić. Ešo was a mechanical engineer, who earned his PhD in Germany, and worked his way up to the managing board of Linde AG. He was looking after markets in the People's Republic of China and Japan. Sometime before coming to Tokyo, Ešo was teaching Thermodynamics in Minneapolis and in Ankara, Turkey. He had a US green card, and eventually both of them were naturalized here.

The other couple were Mahir and Mirsada Hadžiahmetović. He was a representative of the Yugoslav Chamber of Commerce and was really working hard to get some exports going from his homeland, which included building in the Adriatic sea a sea cucumber farm. Sea cucumbers are a delicacy in China and Japan, as my friend Joe Ciasullo can attest from his time in Peking. Later, Mahir became the Bosnian Ambassador to the OECD, whilst Mirsada started and ran a wood processing plant in Bosnia.

Then, there was Boris Vlajčić, a most charming character, born to a German mother and a Croatian father. He was shipped off for education to a Swiss lyceum, studied economy in Paris, and got his first job in Algeria. At the age of 22, he spoke six European languages, and Arabic, fluently. Then he added

Hebrew and in Japan, Japanese. He was the representative of Companie d'Eau, a large French conglomerate. Later, he decided to start facilitating investment groups, targeting Spain, Croatia, Tajikistan, and eventually Vietnam. It was a downward spiral, and at the end of the day, he died broke and alone, having had his Japanese wife divorce him.

Another couple we met were Mita and Erika Arslanagić. Mita, upon Croatia's achievement of independence, became the first Croatian Ambassador to Japan. Erika was a medical doctor on leave from the Croatian Institute of Immunology. Of the non-Yugoslavs, besides Juan Carlos, our closest friends were the Casanovas. Lui was my predecessor in the Joint Venture, and he and Suzy stayed behind for a short period after we arrived. Suzy and Jadranka were very close and that relationship carried over once all of us came back to the States.

THE OTHER OBSERVATION, specifically valid for the US, was how easy it was to get assimilated into the society here. In the beginning, there were occasional jokes about "The Commies are coming", but they were good natured. None of the local employees working for me ever displayed even a hint of objection to being managed by a foreigner. Nor was it ever an issue with various management appointments. Something like that, one would hardly find in good old Europe forty years ago. When foreign managers appeared in European companies, it made headlines. Like Carlos Ghosn, a Lebanese-Brazilian with Renault, or Bjorn Rosengren with ABB in Zürich. Now that the EU has matured a bit, expat managers are not news anymore. But in many places xenophobia continues to exist. Not so in America, the melting pot.

16

LIFE AFTER DEATH

Once out of Unisys, I started to look for a new job, but all the offers came from far away, from unattractive places with one exception, DEC in Boston. Eventually, I decided that maybe a full circle is in order and that I don't have to work, at least for some time. Our social life, now that I did not have to be absent from home any more, became more active. Boris and Juan Carlos would visit from Washington, and we would often go there. And, as one of the pictures shows, we did have some nice dinner parties at home.

From left: Suzi Casanova, Joe Ciasullo, Vicki Harris, Lui, Jadranka, Juan Carlos, Boris, Roger Harris, Lorraine and self

WE ALSO DECIDED to take a long trip south, to the Keys then a visit with Juan Carlos in Paraguay. We did an entire winter of skiing, and eventually I settled for my first love, sailing. Most of my life, from the age of 7, I was sailing, and for some part had also owned a boat. I managed to sail as a guest or charter in the Caribbean, South Africa, Australia, Los Angeles, San Francisco, Solent, the English Channel in the UK, Rio de Janeiro, Rhodes and Corfu, Hawaii, and the Sea of Japan. In other words, almost all the continents, barring Antarctica.

The closest I came to Antarctica was rounding Cape Horn on a cruise ship. But I never had time to spend real time on a boat, rather than a weekend, or a week or two here and there. For a couple of years I did own a sloop in

Split on the Adriatic coast, then another one in Hong Kong, when I was there for the second time. I was in a partnership with Ike Ambrose, Lt.Cmdr. USNR, sailing a 41 ft. Formosa ketch.

> Ike was a great guy. Hated sailing, loved boating. He was a retired nuclear submarine engineer, and on the sailboat, he volunteered to again be an engineer. On the other hand, his wife Cindy, loved sailing, so we flip-flopped. His shift, we would be motoring, my shift we would sail.
>
> On this heavy boat we did some racing. We entered the annual Macau races, always arriving among the last, and exploring surrounding waters east of Hong Kong. Once we went a bit too far into Chinese waters, and almost got arrested by the People's Navy Patrol boat. At that time, I was flying a Yugoslav tricolor with the red star, as the captain's flag. It must have confused the hell out of the Chinese and fortunately they let us go. It was a night navigation, Ike (the Naval Academy guy) was navigating, I was at the wheel. I never let him forget that. In any case, we did not, like some of the other Royal Hong Kong Yacht Club members, spend time in Canton, writing and rewriting apologies for trespassing into the People's paradise.

ONCE WE REALIZED that there is life after death, Jadranka and I decided to attack boating full time. After chartering sailboats in the Chesapeake, it became clear that a powerboat would be a more suitable vessel there. Every sailor eventually migrates to power. More comfort is one reason.

Our first boat, a Marine Trader 38' came with air conditioning. What a luxury compared to those days sitting in the cockpit of a sailboat in the glaring sun, waiting for a breeze. Then there were all the electronic gadgets, including LORAN, an antiquity more for dating the boat than navigating by it.

But the space! The main cabin, guest cabin, living area, galley, two heads, even a bathtub were absolute luxuries. Cruising the Chesapeake became a great pastime. At the beginning, we used Michener's book "Chesapeake", as a guide to exploring the bay. The Chesapeake Bay has some 150 major rivers and over 100,000 smaller tributaries, all to be explored.

A few years later, after taking only a small bite out of the Chesapeake task, we decided that winters in the freezing northern ports, should be avoided and spent in the southern part of the country. We purchased a new boat. We chose a single engine, long range Willard 40 FBS. Trips south, from our home port in Kent, are seven-month adventures. Once committed, there is no chance for return until after the ice is gone. You have to leave before the icing starts, but, for insurance purposes, after the hurricane season is over, around November 30th.

The upper arbitrary insurance border is the Albemarle Sound, so everybody starts sailing south and wait to jump the threshold on the 1st of December. From there on all is fine. No more iced decks, or snow or sleet which the wipers cannot fight. Maybe, through N. Carolina a bit of occasional heating is required, but in general it's paradise. Here we come. We "suffered" through choices of restaurants to visit, fish to eat, and maritime museums along the route to see.

The first time around we spent a good time in the Gulf of Mexico. The next time around, we spent more time on the east coast of Florida. All was not always great. On one trip I contracted bladder cancer, on the other a detached retina.

The last boat, another ADRIA (Symbol 45), came in 2008 brimming with comfort and electronics. It had a full kitchen-size fridge and freezer, washer/dryer, A/C systems, satellite antenna, dinghy hoist, generator, stabilizers, rear view camera, GPS, radar, ALS, two anchors with windlasses, and yes, it did have engines.

ADRIA anchored in Wye river, a resort area of the "All the Elian, all the time", fame

So, we did one more trip south, and eventually gave up on boating. The plan to circumnavigate the eastern side of the US – the East Coast, Great Lakes and down the mighty Mississippi, to Gulf of Mexico, never got a chance. Before we could start planning – and a lot of planning is involved for some 24 months of total time, Jadranka was diagnosed with stage IV cancer and underwent chemo- and radio-therapy. It would not be a good time for her to be in the sun, or on a boat, away from medical facilities. Jadranka passed away, two years after having been initially diagnosed, in September of 2012, and a chapter of 37 years came to an end.

17

POST-JADRANKA

Jadranka passed away amid the commemoration of the 10th anniversary of the attack on the Twin Towers and the Pentagon. 9/11, is an easy date to remember. I think we had a nice service of remembrance for her. All of our local friends came. My sister Koka came from Zagreb, the Liebergots from Washington, and the Harrises from South Carolina. Our boating friends from the Chesapeake area came as well. Fred Davies, who already wasn't in good shape and would regrettably follow her soon, came from London. I really appreciated that. He loved Jadranka and made the trip, which definitely wasn't easy for him. And once everybody left, the house was empty.

After the memorial I did the best thing I thought I could do, I left for a trip to Europe. I went to Zagreb, spent Christmas with family in Genève, as Norman's and

Vera's guest, and the New Year with Fred and Malina in London.

But, when I came back, the house was still empty. So, I visited the local flying school to take up flying airplanes. Although I have a maritime captains' and navigator's license (actually two), and an engineering background, at my age there was not much enthusiasm in getting me in the air. I also had a 1 million miles flown on Pan Am / United, but that didn't help either. They thought I should maybe focus on chess.

My next trip was to the BMW dealership. They were having some type of German festival time, and great deals on bikes were being offered. I hadn't ridden a motorbike for decades, but kept my Croatian and Japanese licenses current. The hungry salesman couldn't care less that he couldn't read any of the two licenses, he'd do anything to close the sale. But I got scared of the machines. It had 1,200 cc, 123 hp, GPS, AM/FM radio, heated handlebars, cruise control, electric lifting of the front shield, radiocommunication with co-pilot and biker-to-biker, and 531 lbs. (241 kg) curb weight. Who would ever be able to lift that?

The deal was killed after a friend gave me a Consumer Guide showing the results of tests of various bikers' clothing. So, for example, falling on asphalt, while wearing jeans, would result in losing all the skin and flesh after skidding for just 30 feet. Not surprisingly, the bikers are called "spare parts" and often they are indeed used as such.

Tessa with the matchmaker, Natalie Bubanj in foreground

HAVING LOOKED at and abandoned more extreme options, I decided to go for the summer, to the house in Dubrovnik. But not before I was introduced by friends (Radovan and Natalie) to a lovely lady, who would eventually become my wife. It turned out that Tessa and I had many things in common from our past.

If I were superstitious, I may have become suspicious. Both of us were widowers. Her husband Bob had passed away a year earlier than Jadranka. For both of us, the death of our respective partners ended our second marriages. We both were childless. Also, Tessa's father and my father were born in the same year, 1906. Tessa's mother and my mother were born in the same year, 1912. We both originated from a Slavic country, Tessa from Ukraine, me from Croatia, and we both emigrated to North America. Tessa to Canada, me to th US.

We both loved math, and we both spent extended time in the same countries, albeit not at the same time. We both lived for some time in France, Hong Kong, Japan, Germany, India, and Australia. We both had families in the former Yugoslavia. Her cousins were in Vrbas in Serbia and in Zagreb, from the time when Ukrainian priests were sent to various countries to spread the Eastern rites Catholicism.

I went to INSEAD and Wharton School, where Tessa's husband Bob was teaching, but not at the time when I was there. On the balance, there were also some differences. She liked small sports cars like the hard to squeeze in, BMW Z3. She didn't sail, she didn't swim, and she gave up skiing ages ago.

18

A NEW ERA. MOVING TO GOD'S WAITING ROOM.

Tessa came to visit me in Lozica that summer. After that, we started spending more and more time together. We traveled through Croatia and through Florida, where she had an apartment. I never thought that I would be able to live in Florida. But, never say never. We married in 2015, and had a nice ceremony in Devon, Pennsylvania, and then another one for our families in Zagreb.

A NEW ERA. MOVING TO GOD'S WAITING ROOM.

Our wedding, on a beautiful day in August

While this was going on, I was remodeling my kitchen in Devon. Tessa was remodeling her kitchen in Philadelphia, and then we jointly continued the remodeling business. Next came splitting her Florida apartment in two, and remodeling the first one, then the second one. When that was done, Tessa sold the two places and we bought a bigger one, which needed, guess what? A kitchen remodeling.

Approach to Surfside in Florida – our winter home

To recover from various remodelings, we spent time on a cruise ship which was something I'd done only once before. I liked running my own boat, not being a passenger. But with a promise of enough pampering, one can change one's mind.

So, we did the Baltics, out of the UK. The next time we cruised from Buenos Aires around the Cape Horn, to Chile. Then out of Singapore, we cruised to Cambodia, Vietnam and Hong Kong. Most Christmases we did short Caribbean weekend cruises with friends, or on our own out of Miami. It sure saved tree-decorating and Christmas cooking.

I got myself an electric scooter, went skiing and was about to have a big bash for my 76th birthday. And then, the pandemic hit. We are locked up, and this writing was born.

We are still discussing whether to make Florida our permanent home. There are many advantages like no state income tax, low energy cost, especially compared to Pennsylvania, and very good and modern medical facilities due to all the insurance money coming with the retirees from up north. Some disadvantages are the extreme heat and humidity from the end of May through September, hurricane exposure, and the need to learn another language. For the time being, we are keeping the house in Pennsylvania, and are hunkering down in Florida, hoping for the Chinese virus to go away. We Will see what the future brings. Who knows, there may be more kitchens to be remodeled.

To quote Churchill again: "It was great fun writing a book – one lived with it." And yes, I thoroughly enjoyed the time I spent writing down my memories.

Surfside, FL, Spring of 2020
raoulmf@aol.com

TIMELINE

- 1893 Grandparents, Hinko and Gizela, married in Zagreb, CRO
- 1899 Aunt Feodora born in Sosnowice, Poland
- 1900 Uncle Raoul C. born in Zürich, Switzerland
- 1902 Aunt Erna born in Zürich, Switzerland
- 1906 Father Ernst Hinko born in Nüremberg, Germany
- 1914 Fischer family interned in Russia
- 1933 Father on the first Lufthansa mail flight over Atlantic
- 1937 Most of the family moves to Zagreb
- 1938 Father moves to Zagreb
- 1943 Father and Ivana Vlahović, my Mother, marry in Zagreb
- 1944 Raoul M. born in Zagreb

- 1952 Father marries Vlasta Ritiř
- 1957 Father divorces Vlasta
- 1962 Raoul enrolls into college, father leaves for Austria
- 1965/66 Military service in Bosanski Brod In Bosnia
- 1968 Mother Ivana dies in traffic accident
- 1968 Raoul marries Miljenka Stanković and gets a first job with IBM-Intertrade in Zagreb
- 1972 Raoul joins Sperry Univac AG in Zurich, as Territory Mgr.
- 1974 Raoul moves to Sperry European HQ in UK, on assignment in London and Amsterdam
- 1975 Raoul and Miljenka divorce.
- 1975 Raoul appointed GM of Yugoslav operations
- 1977 Raoul and Jadranka Kerner get married
- 1978 Raoul appointed GM of Sperry South East Asia Ops., HKG
- 1982 Raoul joins US operation, as Marketing Director
- 1984 Raoul returns to Hong Kong to run PRC and HKG ops
- 1986 Raoul moves to Tokyo, becomes COO of JV, Nippon Univac
- 1990 Raoul moves to Blue Bell, PA as divisional Marketing and Development VP
- 1993 Raoul and Jadranka became American citizens

- 1993 Father dies in Graz, Austria
- 1993 Raoul retires from Unisys Corp
- 2012 Jadranka dies from cancer
- 2015 Tessa and Raoul marry in Devon, PA

FAMILY TREE
Three generations of Raoul M. Fischer family tree

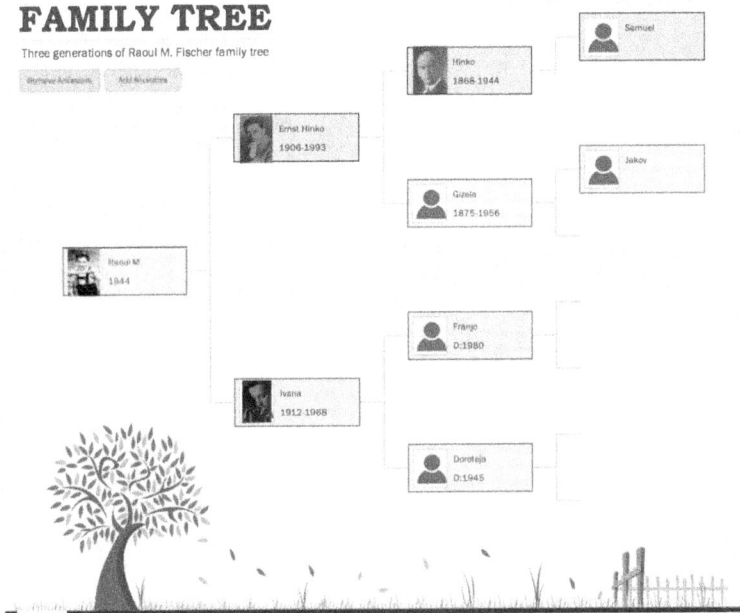

MAPS

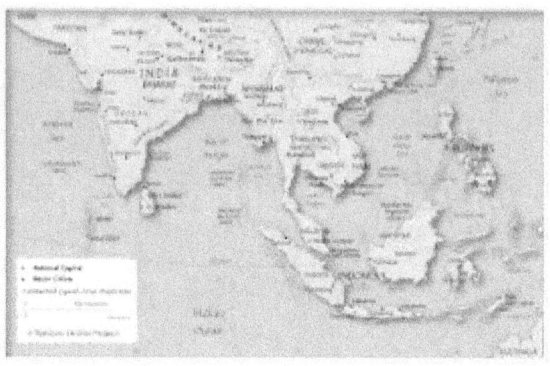

Boundaries:

- To the east – India
- To the south – Indonesia
- To the southwest – Philippines
- To the North – PRC

Operations:

- Hong Kong: Sperry Corp. Ltd. Wholly owned sub.
- New Delhi, India: ORG sales agent
- Singapore: Sperry Univac Pty Ltd.
- Manila, Philippines: Ray Guevara Group
- Taipei, Republic of China: R. King's Distributorship, part of CY Tung's group
- Kuala Lumpur, Malaysia: ON–LINE Sdn. Bhd.
- Bangkok, Thailand: SAMMIT distributorship
- Peking, PRC: direct marketing

Map of European movement of the Fischer family

1. Probitz, Moravia, today Czechia -- Grandfather Hinko's birthplace
2. Sosnowice, Poland – aunt Feodora's birthplace
3. Zürich, Switzerland – uncle Raoul's and aunt Erna's birthplace

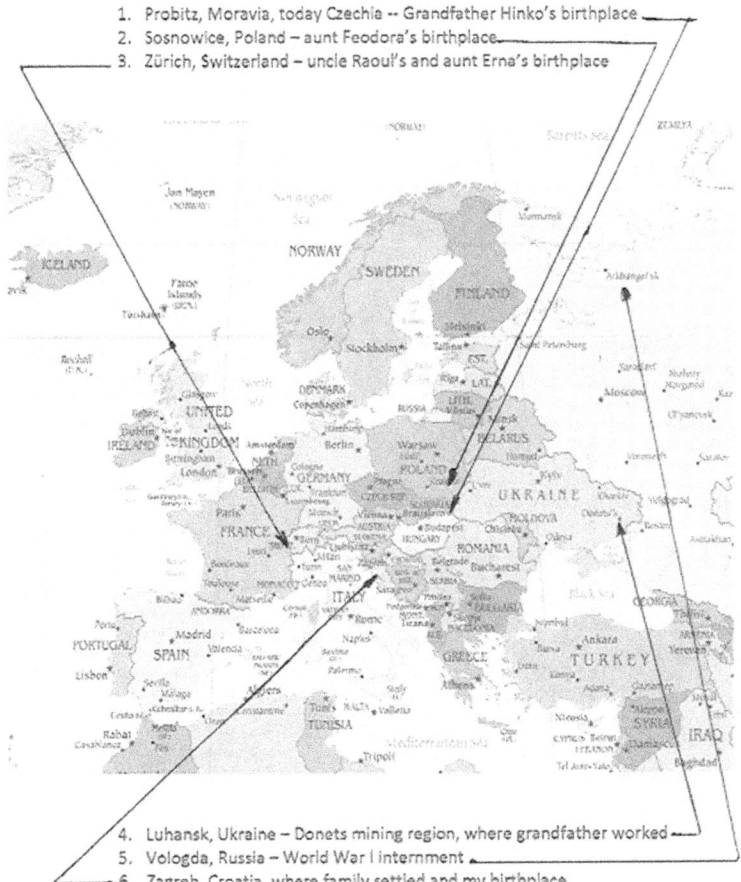

4. Luhansk, Ukraine – Donets mining region, where grandfather worked
5. Vologda, Russia – World War I internment
6. Zagreb, Croatia, where family settled and my birthplace

INDEX OF NAMES

Ambrose Isiah, Ike

Sailing buddy, American naval officer, retired in Australia. His wife Cindy passed away a few years before Jadranka. You want a conservative friend? After retirement, he wouldn't even move back to the States, because the place was "too liberal".

Blažić Metzner Boris

Croatian-Venezuelan originally an agricultural expert, trained in Venezuela and the States, later head of the statistical unit of the World Bank. My friend of our friend Maja, through whom we got introduced, spent a lot of time together in Washington. Passed away in 2013, in Paraguay

Blumenthal W. Michael

Princeton professor, Ambassador, onetime Chairman of Unisys, retired as a Director of the Jewish Museum in Berlin.

Braun Reto

President of Unisys at the time I returned to the States, a Swiss allergic to cheese. Upon return to Switzerland was for a short period in charge of Swiss Telecom

Brkich Slavko S.

We met Slavko and his wife Victoria in Philadelphia, during the war in Croatia. A real-estate developer, two sons. One, Steven, American educated lawyer, was Croatian Premier's adviser, and stayed in Croatia, now in private business. When not in Devon, we spent a lot of time with them on their farm in northern Pennsylvania and their summer home in Cancun, Mexico. Slavko was my Best man

Bubanj Radovan

A Zagreb medical doctor. Father Remigi was director of the University Clinic Rebro, and we had a bunch of common friends, including Predrag Keros. Predrag was a sort of Radovan's Godfather, looking after his career after his father passed away. We even went to the same dancing school together. Radovan's wife Natalie was a friend of Tessa (my future wife) and did some matchmaking on her behalf. Today, Radovan and Natalie also live in Florida, few blocks away from us.

Casanova Luciano and Sue

Friends from way back, spent time together in Japan and PA. Whilst Lui was *l' Italiano vero*, she was of Croatian background, but both Californians. Upon return, we were neighbors for some thirty years.

Ciasullo Joseph C. and Lorraine

At one point of time, Joe was my boss. Also, a neighbor in Valley Forge, and we spent, over the period of almost forty years, a lot of time together. I always made a point, when visiting the HQ in the States, to contact Joe and his wife Lorraine, plus some other friends, so we stayed in touch, despite our absence for many years. He had the bad luck of me involving him in the China business

Crnić Ivana, Ivka, née Vlahović

My mother, died in 1968. Whilst the family came from Zlatar, she was born in Zagreb, one of four girls and four boys. Her youngest sister, Marija (teta Beba), is my source of some family information

Crnić Ružica, Koka

My sister retired, living in Zagreb, with her daughter Tamara. The son Igor is presently in the UK. Her Ukrainian connection is that she married Vlado Gopurenko, whose family hails from Ukraine.

Crnić Želimir

My half-brother, living in Zagreb, with wife Ivanka.

Crnić Zvonko

Came at the end of the war from the partisan resistance as a young man, married my mother, worked as a bartender, and, in his late forties decided to get education for better job prospects. Enrolled in School of Economics, and upon getting a degree, was later director of finances of various industrial outfits in Zagreb

Davies Frederick G.

My boss, my friend

Davies Malina, née Kordić

Fred's widow, Jadranka's friend, now living between the UK and Croatia. Originally emigrated to Canada with a daughter and husband, Branko Krpan, came back, minus husband – Winnipeg was far too cold for a warm-blooded Croatian lady. Later met Fred in Zagreb.

Delalić Bose Zdenka

My colleague at the University. She left Yugoslavia for Vienna (DEC) and later for the US (Westinghouse). Did her PhD at Temple and became a professor there. Married to Glenn Bose, a professor of economy at the American University and has two children.

Ellis James and Zdenka

In the seventies, Jim worked for Fred Davies in Slovenia, and later he was my Ljubljana Branch manager. He left for the Far East, and ended up as my manager for South Asia. He and Zdeni (his Slovene wife), had two daughters, one regrettably with Down syndrome. Little Ana is a well-functioning young lady, whilst the elder daughter, Sandra became a coal mining engineer, thoroughly impressing her father and everybody else around her.

Fischer Ernst Hinko

My father, Pelja

Fischer Gizela, née Rosenthal (Ružinski)

My grandmother, Academy of Music grad, once a year we would hear her playing piano and violin concertos with Raoul, when he would be visiting from England.

Fischer Hinko

My grandfather, died in Zagreb in 1944

Fischer Jadranka, née Kerner

My second wife (1977 – 2012), graduated English German and Italian languages at the University of Zagreb, worked as a librarian in IBM, where I first met her, and later moved to Univac, where we got together.

Fischer Miljenka, née Stanković

My first wife, an architect and a future urban designer. We divorced in 1975

Fischer Ignaz, Naci

My father's uncle, architect who built majority of the capital buildings in Zagreb

Fischer Sartorius Feodora, Fedja

My aunt, pediatrician, director of a children's hospital (that uncle Naci built) and a Center for protection of mother and child – a UNICEF project

Fischer Vlasta, née Rytiř

My father's second wife, 1952 to 1958. Her Czech parents, had a large flower growing business in Sarajevo, until the Communists confiscated the land (and built the Koševo hospital complex – that made them feel good). Vlasta was a singer on Zagreb radio station. Later, she took a job in my father's factory, where they got together. Her parents eventually moved to Dubrovnik, bought a house on the shore, and restarted the flower business. I spent all the summers there, mostly sailing, and ministering in the church on Sundays.

Fisher Raoul C.

My uncle. Since before WWII living in London, mechanical, petroleum, nuclear engineer. While visiting him, I was treated as a son, by both him, and his wife Dorothy

Harris Roger and Vicki

A colleague from the company used to see a lot of them in the eighties and nineties, it cooled off, and revived a bit when they came for Jadranka's memorial in 2012. Live in Beaufort, SC.

House Fischer Taisa, née Vanio

Tess, my third wife, high school math teacher, Canadian, born in Ukraine

Hrase von Bargen, Juan Carlos A.

Boris Blažić's partner, Minister in the Paraguayan Embassy in Washington and later Ambassador of Paraguay to Japan. Spent many years socializing and travailing together in Japan, US, Croatia, Paraguay. Retired now in PY

Huber Erna, née Fischer

Father's second sister, who came to Zagreb with her daughters, Ursi Maier-Brügeman married Doder, and Heidi, married Šporčić

Ivanović Viktor

A friend from the college days, later we worked together for Univac, Spent some family vacations together on the Adriatic coast. He was my best men in my second marriage to Jadranka

Iveković Darko

IBM manager, friend from before me joining the company, my first manager. Living in Zagreb, with wife Melita

Keros Predrag

Another one of friends of my cousin, whom we met often whilst still in Zagreb, and then later on my visits from overseas. Medical professor and Dean of the School of medicine. Orthopedic- and neurosurgeon. Combined popularization of medical science and serious research, and is known for Keros classification. Wife Jadranka, from Dubrovnik, schoolmate of my wife, was later Dean of the Dental College.

Kljaković Vida, née Tućan

Originally, a friend of my cousins, Norman and Ursi, I inherited her after both Ursi and Norman left Yugoslavia. She married Darko, and later Vanča

Kljaković, a well-known Yugoslav theatre and cinema director and playwright. She was a master of scenography, knitwear and home décor. Had several solo art exhibitions. Very active in NGOs, helping displaced women following the war in Croatia

Koren Vilko

Childhood friend since 1952, now living with wife Marija, two daughters and a grandchild Oskar, in Slovenia. Once retired, he turned into professional-grade photographer

Liebergot Harris

Friend from Japan times, where he was on the NUL board and helped me navigate the Japanese labyrinths of culture and language. Impressed everybody when after retiring from Unisys, he went for a PhD to Drexel U. We still see him, and his wife Bonnie, from time to time.

Makarović Berislav, Makar

Makar, and his now former wife Zdravka, we inherited from Norman, when he left Yugoslavia. Film and TV director, with a couple of nice films and TV series in his portfolio. After all these years, we still see him every time we visit Zagreb

Mršić Zdravko

My first manager whilst in IBM marketing, later joined me in the Far East, and ended his career as the Minister of Foreign Affairs of Republic of Croatia

Muftić Osman

One more of Norman's friends with whom we stayed in contact. Originally, he was teaching at the School of Mechanical Engineering, eventually became the Dean of the School, and for a short stint, the Ambassador of Croatia to the Republic of Iran

Ružinski René

My father's cousin, friend and business partner. Retired as a Consul General of Kingdom of Norway and the Doyen of the Corps Consulaire in Zagreb (had at least 30 years of seniority over any of the other consuls there

Sartorius Fritz

Father of Norman's, professor of medicine, stayed behind in Germany after the racial rules forced his divorce with Feodora. He settled In East Germany, where he was running a biology institute. Had two sons, one, Frank, we met in Berlin. Fritz came to Zagreb once, in the 1960-es, for a visit.

Sartorius Norman H., (NS5)

My cousin, medical professor, psychiatrists, phycologist, former director of WHO Mental Health Unit, today called the most important psychiatrist in the world and a living legend (by Lancet). With his wife Vera, my colleague and additionally, an archeologist, he lives in Genève.

Sartorius Vera, née Pecikozić

Norman's wife, we studied together the two initial years of college. She is a graduate electrical engineer and later she graduated Archeology in Genève.

Springstead E. T., Ted

Was for a short period VP running several organizations in Europe, later in Asia, and eventually corporate business in PRC, representing all Sperry divisions. Was twice my boss, last in 1980.

Vlahović Josip

My uncle, Yugoslav resistance hero, head of Croatian Communist Youth movement, executed 1941

www.ingramcontent.com/pod-product-compliance
Lightning Source LLC
Chambersburg PA
CBHW060104230426
43661CB00033B/1409/J